MICROSERVICES DESIGN PATTERNS
FOR SERVERLESS APPLICATION

Unlocking Scalable Solutions: Mastering Design Patterns for
High-Performance Serverless Microservices

SIMON TELLIER

TABLE OF CONTENTS

TABLE OF CONTENTS

CHAPTER 1: INTRODUCTION TO MICROSERVICES AND SERVERLESS ARCHITECTURES

1.1 Understanding Microservices

Microservices architecture represents a shift away from traditional monolithic designs, where an application is built as a single, tightly integrated unit. Instead, microservices break down an application into smaller, independent, and loosely coupled services that each focus on a specific business function. Each microservice can be developed, deployed, and scaled independently, making it easier to manage large applications with diverse requirements.

In essence, microservices enable teams to work on different parts of an application simultaneously, improving productivity and reducing deployment time. This modular approach is ideal for large, complex systems that require flexibility, scalability, and resilience.

Each microservice typically communicates with other microservices through lightweight protocols, such as RESTful APIs or messaging queues. These services often use different technologies and can be written in various programming languages. Microservices also interact with databases, which can be managed individually for each service (the "database per service" pattern). This approach contrasts sharply with monolithic systems, where a single database is typically shared by all components of the application.

The key principle behind microservices is **decentralization**. By decentralizing both data management and functionality, microservices improve scalability and fault tolerance. If one service fails, it doesn't necessarily bring down the entire system, allowing for more robust and reliable applications.

1

A crucial advantage of microservices is their ability to be deployed independently. This independent deployment makes it easier to update and scale each service without disrupting others. If a specific service needs an update or scaling, developers can make those changes without affecting the rest of the application. This provides greater agility and faster time to market, as updates can be rolled out incrementally.

As organizations scale their applications, the microservices model also makes it easier to incorporate continuous integration/continuous delivery (CI/CD) pipelines. This further enhances the development lifecycle by automating testing, integration, and deployment, ensuring faster and more reliable software releases.

In the context of serverless architectures, microservices have become even more powerful. Serverless computing provides a way to run microservices without managing the underlying infrastructure. Serverless platforms, such as AWS Lambda, Google Cloud Functions, and Azure Functions, automatically scale applications up or down based on demand, which aligns perfectly with the modularity and flexibility of microservices. Serverless also simplifies many aspects of microservice management, such as auto-scaling and load balancing, making it an attractive choice for modern application development.

1.2 Key Benefits of Microservices

Microservices bring several key benefits to application development, particularly in organizations that are striving to build scalable, resilient, and agile systems. Here's a deeper dive into the advantages of adopting a microservices-based architecture:

1. **Scalability and Flexibility** One of the most significant advantages of microservices is the ability to scale services independently. In traditional monolithic systems, scaling requires duplicating the entire application, which can be resource-intensive and inefficient. With microservices, you can scale only the specific services that require additional resources, optimizing both performance and cost.

For instance, if a service handling user authentication experiences high demand, it can be scaled up independently of other services like order processing or inventory management. This granular control over scaling allows businesses to optimize their infrastructure resources and reduce unnecessary costs.

2. **Resilience and Fault Isolation** Microservices architecture is inherently more resilient than monolithic systems. Because each microservice operates independently, a failure in one service does not necessarily impact the others. If a particular microservice goes down, the rest of the application can continue functioning, allowing the system to recover quickly without significant downtime.

   Microservices also make it easier to implement **circuit breakers** and **failover mechanisms**, which help prevent cascading failures. These strategies ensure that even when one service fails, the system as a whole remains operational, enhancing overall fault tolerance.

3. **Faster Development and Deployment** Microservices enable smaller, more manageable codebases, which makes development faster and more efficient. Different teams can work on different services in parallel, reducing bottlenecks and improving collaboration. Developers can also focus on one service at a time, making it easier to troubleshoot and improve specific parts of the application. Moreover, because each service is independent, microservices allow for continuous integration and continuous deployment (CI/CD). Updates to one service can be rolled out without affecting the entire system, leading to faster release cycles and more frequent updates.

4. **Technology Agnosticism** In a microservices architecture, each service can use the most appropriate technology for its task. For example, one microservice might be written in Java for its robustness in enterprise environments, while another might be written in Python for its ease of use in data processing tasks. This flexibility enables teams to adopt the best tools for each part of the application, rather than being limited by the technology stack of a monolithic system. Teams can choose the programming languages, databases, and

frameworks that suit the specific needs of each service, making the overall system more efficient and effective.

5. **Improved Maintenance and Updates** The modularity of microservices makes maintaining and updating applications much easier. In a monolithic system, updating a single component may require rebuilding and redeploying the entire application. In contrast, with microservices, each service can be updated independently, allowing for continuous improvement without disrupting the entire application.

   This modularity also makes it easier to isolate and fix bugs, as developers can focus on the specific service that is malfunctioning, rather than dealing with a large, complex monolithic codebase.

6. **Easier Scaling of Teams** Microservices enable organizations to scale development teams more easily. Each service can be developed by a small, specialized team that focuses on a specific domain. These teams can work in parallel, leading to faster development and the ability to scale resources and efforts as needed.

   This decentralized approach also reduces the communication overhead that often exists in large, monolithic teams, making it easier for developers to manage their tasks and focus on specific challenges.

1.3 What Is Serverless?

Serverless computing is a cloud-computing model that allows developers to build and run applications without managing servers. In traditional computing models, developers are responsible for provisioning, scaling, and maintaining the infrastructure needed to run applications. However, serverless computing abstracts away these tasks, enabling developers to focus solely on writing code and developing business logic.

The term "serverless" is somewhat misleading because servers are still involved. What it really refers to is the abstraction of server management from the developer. Serverless platforms, such as AWS Lambda, Azure Functions, and Google Cloud Functions,

4

automatically handle the infrastructure, scaling, and maintenance, allowing developers to simply deploy their functions and let the platform manage the rest.

In serverless computing, developers write **functions**, which are small pieces of code that perform a specific task. These functions are executed in response to events, such as HTTP requests, file uploads, or database updates. Serverless platforms automatically allocate resources for each function when it is triggered and scale up or down as needed based on demand. This means you only pay for the computing time your code actually uses, rather than for idle server capacity.

One of the main advantages of serverless is **cost efficiency**. With traditional infrastructure, you pay for a fixed amount of computing resources regardless of whether they're used or not. In a serverless model, however, you pay only for the execution time of your code, which can significantly reduce costs, especially for applications with fluctuating or unpredictable workloads.

Another benefit is **auto-scaling**. Serverless platforms automatically scale applications up or down in response to demand, without any input from the developer. If an application experiences a sudden spike in traffic, the serverless platform will automatically add more resources to handle the increased load. When the demand decreases, the platform will scale back down, reducing costs.

Serverless computing is also highly **event-driven**. Functions are triggered by specific events, such as changes in a database, HTTP requests, or even messages from other services. This event-driven nature is well-suited to modern applications, where many processes are asynchronous and rely on real-time data. Serverless platforms integrate easily with other cloud services, making it possible to build highly interconnected applications that respond to real-time events with minimal latency.

Moreover, serverless platforms reduce the operational overhead for developers, as they no longer need to worry about server provisioning, patching, or scaling. This allows teams to focus on delivering business value rather than managing infrastructure.

5

Serverless also offers high **availability**. Because the cloud provider automatically manages the infrastructure, applications built on serverless platforms benefit from the provider's fault tolerance and high availability features, including automatic retries and failover mechanisms.

While serverless computing offers many benefits, it's important to recognize its limitations as well. Serverless applications are typically designed for stateless workloads, and maintaining state across function invocations can be challenging. Additionally, functions may have execution time limits, which could be a drawback for long-running processes. Finally, while serverless platforms handle scaling and infrastructure management, they may not offer the same level of fine-grained control over infrastructure as traditional server-based solutions.

Overall, serverless computing provides a streamlined, efficient way to build and deploy applications, making it a compelling option for modern cloud-based microservices architectures. It eliminates much of the operational overhead associated with traditional server management, enabling developers to focus on building scalable, cost-effective applications that respond quickly to user demands.

1.4 How Serverless Enhances Microservices

Serverless computing and microservices complement each other perfectly, offering a combination that can greatly simplify the development and deployment of modern applications. While microservices focus on breaking down large, complex applications into smaller, independently deployable services, serverless enhances this modularity by removing the need to manage servers and infrastructure.

Here's how serverless enhances microservices:

1. **Simplified Deployment and Scaling** One of the most significant ways serverless enhances microservices is through simplified deployment and scaling. In a traditional microservices architecture, each microservice requires

infrastructure, scaling mechanisms, and load balancing to be manually managed. With serverless computing, these aspects are handled automatically by the platform.

When a new microservice is deployed on a serverless platform like AWS Lambda, it is automatically scaled according to the workload. If traffic spikes, serverless platforms can quickly allocate more resources to handle the increased demand. Once the traffic decreases, the resources scale back down, ensuring that you only pay for what you use. This seamless auto-scaling takes much of the operational burden off development teams and allows them to focus on writing the code for individual microservices.

2. **Event-Driven Architecture** Serverless computing is inherently event-driven, which aligns well with the microservices pattern. Each microservice typically listens for events, such as API requests, database changes, or messages in a queue. Serverless platforms make it easy to implement this event-driven architecture by automatically triggering functions in response to these events. This is particularly useful in microservices, where each service may need to respond to different events based on its specific function. For example, one microservice might handle user authentication, while another manages order processing. When an event occurs, such as a user logging in or placing an order, the appropriate microservice is triggered to handle the request, making the system highly reactive and adaptable.

3. **Faster Time to Market** Serverless computing streamlines the development lifecycle by removing the need for developers to worry about provisioning, managing, and scaling infrastructure. Developers can focus solely on building the individual microservices themselves, leading to faster deployment times. This, in turn, reduces the time to market for new features and updates. Because serverless platforms abstract away many of the operational tasks, microservices can be developed and deployed in parallel, further speeding up the development process. Teams can work independently on different services, pushing out changes or new features without affecting the rest of the application.

This enables faster iteration and more frequent updates, essential for staying competitive in today's fast-paced software landscape.

4. **Cost Efficiency** Serverless computing is cost-effective, especially when combined with microservices. In traditional server-based architectures, organizations often have to provision and manage a large number of servers, paying for them even when they're not in use. With serverless, you only pay for the execution time of each individual microservice, which is highly cost-efficient for unpredictable workloads.

   In a microservices architecture, each service can be optimized for cost based on its specific usage patterns. For example, a service that experiences high traffic can be allocated more resources, while a service with sporadic traffic can scale down during low-demand periods. Serverless platforms make it easy to implement these cost-saving strategies without manual intervention.

5. **Improved Fault Isolation** One of the key principles of microservices is fault isolation, meaning that the failure of one service should not impact the rest of the system. Serverless architectures enhance this principle by allowing microservices to run in isolated environments with automatic failover mechanisms.

   If one microservice fails in a serverless system, it can be restarted without impacting other services. Furthermore, many serverless platforms offer automatic retries, ensuring that failed requests are reattempted until they succeed. This level of fault tolerance makes serverless microservices highly resilient and minimizes the impact of errors on the overall application.

6. **Simplified Management** Serverless platforms manage much of the operational overhead, such as provisioning servers, patching, and scaling. This allows development teams to spend more time focusing on the business logic of their microservices rather than worrying about managing infrastructure.

   Serverless platforms also make it easier to implement monitoring and logging for microservices. Most serverless platforms come with built-in tools for tracking function performance, logging errors, and viewing usage metrics. This centralized management and monitoring make it easier to identify and resolve issues, improving the reliability of the entire system.

1.5 Why Serverless Architecture?

The serverless computing model offers a compelling alternative to traditional server-based architectures, particularly for modern application development. Here are some key reasons why organizations are choosing serverless architectures for their applications:

1. **No Server Management** One of the most significant advantages of serverless architecture is the removal of server management. With traditional server-based setups, developers must provision, configure, and maintain servers, handle capacity planning, and ensure that the infrastructure is running smoothly. Serverless platforms eliminate the need for developers to manage servers, freeing them from tasks like hardware provisioning, scaling, and maintenance. This allows developers to focus entirely on writing code and building features.

2. **Cost-Effectiveness** Serverless computing is highly cost-efficient because you only pay for the actual compute resources used, rather than for idle server capacity. This pay-as-you-go model is ideal for applications with fluctuating or unpredictable traffic. For example, if a service experiences a sudden spike in traffic, the serverless platform will automatically allocate more resources to handle the load. Once the traffic decreases, the resources scale down, and you only pay for the compute time during that period.

   This cost-efficiency is particularly beneficial for startups or organizations with limited budgets, as they can avoid the significant upfront costs of provisioning and maintaining physical servers.

3. **Faster Development and Deployment** Serverless architectures enable faster development cycles because developers can focus on building the application logic rather than managing the underlying infrastructure. With serverless computing, deploying code is as simple as uploading a function to the cloud, and

updates can be rolled out quickly without disrupting the rest of the application. Serverless also enables continuous integration and continuous deployment (CI/CD), making it easier to automate testing, integration, and deployment. This leads to more frequent releases, quicker bug fixes, and faster time to market for new features.

4. **Scalability** Serverless platforms provide automatic scaling based on the demand for your application. If your service experiences increased traffic, the platform automatically provisions additional resources to handle the load. Conversely, if traffic decreases, the platform scales down, saving costs. This elasticity allows businesses to accommodate variable workloads without having to worry about capacity planning.

   Moreover, serverless platforms can scale services to virtually unlimited capacity, which is particularly useful for applications that experience unpredictable or rapidly growing traffic.

5. **Flexibility and Agility** Serverless computing promotes flexibility and agility because each function or microservice operates independently. This allows for faster experimentation and iteration, as developers can work on different services in parallel and release them independently.

   Furthermore, serverless platforms support a variety of programming languages, databases, and frameworks, allowing teams to choose the best tools for each service. This flexibility is essential for building modern applications that need to adapt to changing business requirements or new technologies.

6. **Built-in High Availability and Fault Tolerance** Serverless platforms are inherently highly available and fault-tolerant. Cloud providers manage the infrastructure, ensuring that applications run smoothly even in the event of hardware failures. Many serverless platforms also offer automatic retries for failed requests, ensuring that services remain operational even if individual functions experience temporary failures.

   The architecture is designed to automatically distribute workloads across multiple servers and regions, reducing the risk of downtime and ensuring that the application is always available to users.

1.6 Key Challenges in Adopting Serverless

While serverless computing offers numerous benefits, there are also challenges to consider when adopting this architecture. Understanding these challenges can help organizations mitigate risks and make informed decisions about when and how to use serverless.

1. **Cold Starts** A cold start occurs when a serverless function is called for the first time after being idle for a period. During this time, the platform must allocate resources and initialize the function, leading to a delay in processing the request. For applications with high latency requirements, cold starts can be a significant issue. While serverless providers are continually working to reduce cold start times, they remain a challenge for certain types of applications.

2. **State Management** Serverless functions are inherently stateless, meaning they do not maintain any information between executions. This makes it difficult to manage state across multiple function invocations. For stateful applications, developers need to implement external state management solutions, such as storing state in databases or using distributed caches. Managing state in serverless architectures requires careful planning and design.

3. **Vendor Lock-In** Serverless computing is often closely tied to specific cloud providers, leading to concerns about vendor lock-in. Once an application is built using a particular serverless platform, it can be difficult to migrate to another provider without significant changes to the code and infrastructure. Organizations must carefully consider the long-term implications of choosing a specific cloud provider for their serverless applications.

4. **Limited Execution Time** Many serverless platforms impose limits on the maximum execution time for functions. For example, AWS Lambda has a default maximum execution time of 15 minutes. For long-running processes,

serverless may not be the best solution, as these functions may need to be broken up into smaller tasks or use alternative architectures, such as containerized solutions.

5. **Complexity in Debugging and Monitoring** Debugging serverless applications can be more complex than traditional applications due to the distributed nature of the architecture. Tracing requests across multiple services, functions, and databases can be challenging, especially as the number of functions grows. Fortunately, most serverless platforms offer built-in monitoring and logging tools to help with debugging, but additional tools and strategies may be required as the application scales.

1.7 Real-World Use Cases of Serverless Microservices

Serverless microservices are increasingly being adopted across industries to solve a wide variety of challenges. Here are some examples of how serverless is being used in real-world applications:

1. **E-Commerce Platforms** Many e-commerce platforms use serverless microservices to handle a wide range of tasks, from user authentication to payment processing. For example, a serverless function could be triggered when a customer places an order, which would initiate the payment process, update inventory levels, and notify the customer—all with minimal infrastructure management.

2. **IoT Applications** Serverless is an excellent fit for Internet of Things (IoT) applications, where devices generate vast amounts of event-driven data. Serverless functions can be used to process this data in real time, triggering other actions such as sending notifications, updating databases, or invoking machine learning models for analysis.

3. **Financial Services** Financial institutions use serverless microservices for tasks such as fraud detection, transaction processing, and compliance monitoring. Serverless enables them to handle high volumes of transactions with low latency,

scale services independently based on demand, and pay only for the compute resources they actually use.

4. **Media and Entertainment** The media industry leverages serverless computing to handle tasks like video encoding, file transcoding, and content distribution. For example, a media platform may use serverless functions to automatically convert video files into multiple formats based on the user's device, ensuring seamless streaming across a variety of platforms.

1.8 The Evolution of Serverless and Microservices

The evolution of serverless and microservices has been driven by the increasing demand for agility, scalability, and cost efficiency in application development. While microservices gained traction as a way to break down large, monolithic applications into smaller, manageable services, serverless computing has further accelerated this shift by removing the burden of infrastructure management.

Initially, microservices were implemented using traditional server-based architectures, requiring developers to provision and manage servers for each microservice. Over time, the rise of cloud computing and containerization technologies like Docker and Kubernetes made it easier to deploy and manage microservices at scale. These technologies allowed microservices to be packaged into containers, enabling better portability and scalability.

Serverless computing represents the next step in the evolution of microservices. With serverless, developers no longer need to worry about managing the infrastructure that supports microservices. Serverless platforms handle all aspects of infrastructure management, allowing developers to focus on writing code and defining business logic. This abstraction enables faster development cycles, reduced operational overhead, and more cost-effective applications.

As serverless platforms continue to mature, they are likely to become an even more integral part of microservices architectures. The combination of serverless and

13

microservices is reshaping how applications are built, deployed, and scaled, offering greater flexibility, resilience, and efficiency. The future of application development will likely see even more innovations in serverless computing, further cementing its role in the evolution of microservices architectures.

Chapter 2: The Building Blocks of Serverless Microservices

2.1 Cloud Platforms for Serverless Applications

Cloud platforms have revolutionized the way software is developed and deployed, especially with the rise of serverless computing. The ability to offload infrastructure management to cloud providers has allowed businesses to focus on writing code and building features rather than worrying about servers, scaling, or provisioning hardware. For serverless applications, cloud platforms are at the heart of the operation, enabling developers to run code in response to events without managing the underlying infrastructure. Let's explore some of the key cloud platforms that provide serverless computing services.

1. **Amazon Web Services (AWS)** AWS is one of the pioneers in the serverless computing space, offering a wide range of services that support serverless architectures. The most well-known AWS serverless service is **AWS Lambda**, which allows developers to run code without provisioning or managing servers. Lambda can be triggered by a variety of events such as HTTP requests, file uploads to S3, database changes in DynamoDB, and more.
   AWS also provides additional services that integrate seamlessly with Lambda to create a fully serverless application:
   - **API Gateway**: Manages API calls and routes them to Lambda functions.
   - **DynamoDB**: A NoSQL database that can trigger Lambda functions on data changes.
   - **S3**: Used for object storage and can trigger Lambda functions when files are uploaded or modified.
   - **SNS** and **SQS**: For event-driven architecture, enabling asynchronous messaging and notifications.

2. AWS also offers **Step Functions**, which allow developers to coordinate Lambda functions into workflows, making it easier to manage complex serverless applications. Additionally, **AWS Fargate** is a container service that simplifies the deployment and management of containers, which can also integrate with serverless architectures for certain use cases.

3. **Google Cloud Platform (GCP)** Google Cloud is another major player in the serverless space. Google's serverless offerings include **Google Cloud Functions**, which is similar to AWS Lambda. It enables developers to write single-purpose functions that respond to events and run in a fully managed environment. Google Cloud Functions can be triggered by HTTP requests, cloud storage events, changes to Cloud Firestore, and more.

    Google Cloud also provides other tools to help implement serverless architectures:

    - **Google Cloud Pub/Sub**: A messaging service that facilitates event-driven communication between microservices.
    - **Firebase**: A platform for building web and mobile applications that integrates seamlessly with Google Cloud Functions for serverless backend services.
    - **Google Cloud Run**: A platform for running containerized applications without managing infrastructure, enabling developers to build and deploy applications that can scale automatically.

4. GCP's serverless offering stands out for its ability to easily integrate with Google's machine learning tools and data processing services, making it an ideal choice for businesses with heavy data processing or AI/ML needs.

5. **Microsoft Azure** Microsoft Azure provides robust support for serverless computing through its **Azure Functions** platform. Similar to AWS Lambda and Google Cloud Functions, Azure Functions lets developers run code in response to events without worrying about the infrastructure. Azure Functions supports multiple programming languages, including C#, JavaScript, Python, and Java, and can be triggered by HTTP requests, database changes, timer events, or

messages from queues.

In addition to Azure Functions, Azure provides several complementary services for building serverless applications:

- **Azure Logic Apps**: A service for automating workflows and integrating with third-party services, which can invoke Azure Functions.
- **Azure Event Grid**: A fully managed event routing service that facilitates event-driven architecture, routing events from various sources to Azure Functions or other services.
- **Cosmos DB**: A globally distributed NoSQL database that integrates with Azure Functions for real-time data processing.

6. Azure's ecosystem also includes support for hybrid architectures, enabling businesses to integrate on-premises systems with cloud-based serverless applications. This flexibility makes Azure a strong contender for enterprises with complex, hybrid needs.

7. **Other Cloud Providers** While AWS, Google Cloud, and Azure dominate the serverless market, other cloud platforms are also offering serverless solutions. For example:

- **IBM Cloud Functions**: Based on Apache OpenWhisk, IBM's serverless platform allows developers to run functions in response to events from various sources.
- **Oracle Cloud Functions**: Oracle offers serverless computing as part of its cloud platform, focusing on scalability and integration with Oracle databases and enterprise applications.

8. As the serverless space continues to grow, these cloud platforms are likely to develop more competitive offerings, making it even easier for developers to choose the best platform for their needs.

Overall, choosing the right cloud platform for serverless applications depends on several factors, including the specific use case, pricing, existing infrastructure, and integrations with other services. AWS, GCP, and Azure provide comprehensive and reliable serverless offerings, while smaller players like IBM Cloud and Oracle offer niche benefits for certain industries or technical requirements.

2.2 Serverless Functions: AWS Lambda, Google Cloud Functions, and Azure Functions

At the core of serverless computing are serverless functions. These functions are the building blocks that respond to events, perform computations, and handle business logic. Each major cloud provider offers its own version of serverless functions, which are central to enabling serverless microservices. Let's take a closer look at the three most prominent serverless function platforms: **AWS Lambda**, **Google Cloud Functions**, and **Azure Functions**.

1. **AWS Lambda** AWS Lambda is one of the most widely used serverless compute services, allowing developers to run their code in response to events. Lambda supports multiple programming languages, including Node.js, Python, Java, Go, Ruby, and C#. Each Lambda function is stateless and runs in response to an event trigger, such as an HTTP request, a file upload to S3, or a message from a queue.
   Key Features of AWS Lambda:
   - ○ **Event-driven:** Lambda can be triggered by events from over 200 AWS services, including S3, DynamoDB, API Gateway, and SNS.
   - ○ **Automatic Scaling:** Lambda automatically scales the number of instances based on the number of incoming requests. It can handle thousands of requests simultaneously.
   - ○ **Resource Management:** You don't need to worry about provisioning servers, as AWS manages all the infrastructure.
   - ○ **Short Execution Time:** Lambda functions can run for up to 15 minutes, making it suitable for short-lived tasks. For longer-running processes, AWS offers other solutions, such as AWS Step Functions.

2. **When to Use AWS Lambda:** AWS Lambda is best suited for microservices, real-time data processing, IoT applications, and event-driven systems. It is also ideal for applications with fluctuating traffic, where the ability to scale dynamically is important.

3. **Google Cloud Functions** Google Cloud Functions is Google's serverless computing platform, designed to handle single-purpose functions that respond to events. It integrates seamlessly with other Google Cloud services like Cloud Pub/Sub, Firebase, and Cloud Storage. Google Cloud Functions supports several programming languages, including Node.js, Python, Go, and Java.

   Key Features of Google Cloud Functions:
   - **Lightweight and Fast:** Cloud Functions are designed to execute quickly and are suitable for handling lightweight, stateless tasks.
   - **Integration with Google Services:** Cloud Functions can be easily integrated with other Google Cloud services like Cloud Pub/Sub, Cloud Firestore, and Cloud Storage, making it ideal for building event-driven applications.
   - **Automatic Scaling:** Like AWS Lambda, Cloud Functions automatically scale based on demand. It can automatically handle thousands of simultaneous events without any manual intervention.

4. **When to Use Google Cloud Functions:** Google Cloud Functions is an excellent choice for businesses heavily invested in the Google Cloud ecosystem or those building event-driven, data-intensive applications that rely on other Google services, like Firebase or BigQuery.

5. **Azure Functions** Azure Functions is Microsoft's serverless compute service that runs code in response to events. It supports multiple languages, including C#, Java, JavaScript, and Python, and integrates with a wide array of Azure services, such as Azure Event Grid, Cosmos DB, and Azure Logic Apps.

   Key Features of Azure Functions:

- Multiple Trigger Sources: Azure Functions can be triggered by a wide variety of events, such as HTTP requests, database changes, message queues, and timers.
- **Development Flexibility:** Azure Functions supports both built-in triggers and custom triggers, providing developers with flexibility in how they architect their event-driven systems.
- **Serverless Hosting Plans:** Azure offers different hosting plans, including the Consumption Plan (pay-as-you-go) and Premium Plan, providing the right balance of cost-efficiency and performance for various use cases.

6. **When to Use Azure Functions:** Azure Functions is ideal for enterprises using Microsoft's suite of products or businesses with hybrid cloud needs. It's also well-suited for organizations that require seamless integration with Microsoft technologies and on-premises systems.

2.3 Event-Driven Architecture Explained

Event-driven architecture (EDA) is an architectural paradigm that revolves around the production, detection, and consumption of events. An **event** is any change in state or occurrence that is significant to the system. For example, in a microservices system, an event could be an HTTP request, a new message in a queue, or an update in a database. The core idea behind EDA is that the system reacts to events by triggering the relevant processes or services that handle those events.

In the context of serverless microservices, event-driven architecture is crucial because serverless platforms like AWS Lambda, Google Cloud Functions, and Azure Functions are designed to respond to events. Here's a deeper dive into the components and benefits of event-driven architecture:

1. **Event Producers** Event producers are the systems or components that generate events. In the context of serverless microservices, event producers could be:

- ○ **User actions** (e.g., clicking a button, submitting a form)
- ○ **External services** (e.g., a payment gateway sending a transaction notification)
- ○ **Internal system events** (e.g., a change in a database record or a file upload to cloud storage)

2. **Event Consumers** Event consumers are the components or services that respond to events. In serverless applications, event consumers are typically serverless functions, such as AWS Lambda, Google Cloud Functions, or Azure Functions. When an event occurs, the appropriate function is triggered to handle that event. For example, a file upload to cloud storage might trigger a function that processes the file and stores it in a database.

3. **Event Channels** Event channels are the communication paths through which events are transmitted. In an event-driven serverless application, event channels could include services like:
   - ○ **Message Queues** (e.g., AWS SQS, Google Cloud Pub/Sub, Azure Service Bus)
   - ○ **Streaming Services** (e.g., AWS Kinesis, Google Cloud Dataflow)
   - ○ **HTTP Requests** (e.g., API Gateway triggers)

4. **Event Sourcing** Event sourcing is a design pattern often used in event-driven architectures, where state changes are stored as a series of events. Instead of directly modifying the state of a system, events are logged, and the current state is rebuilt by processing the event log. This ensures that all changes to the system are recorded and can be replayed if necessary, providing an immutable history of state changes.

5. **Benefits of Event-Driven Architecture in Serverless Microservices**
   - ○ **Decoupling:** Services are loosely coupled in an event-driven system, meaning that the producer of the event does not need to know about the consumers. This increases flexibility and makes it easier to evolve the system over time.

- ○ **Scalability:** Event-driven systems scale easily because new consumers can be added without modifying the event producers. Serverless platforms scale automatically in response to events, ensuring that the system can handle fluctuating demand.
- ○ **Real-time Processing:** EDA is ideal for applications that require real-time processing, such as real-time analytics, notifications, and IoT systems. Serverless functions can be triggered by events as soon as they occur, reducing latency.

By combining serverless computing with event-driven architecture, businesses can build highly scalable, responsive, and cost-effective applications that react to real-time events. This makes event-driven serverless systems ideal for a wide variety of use cases, from IoT applications to financial transactions and beyond.

2.4 API Gateway Integration for Serverless Systems

In modern microservices architectures, particularly those using serverless computing, **API gateways** play a pivotal role in providing a unified entry point to the various services that make up an application. For serverless systems, an API Gateway provides the bridge between the client (e.g., web or mobile application) and serverless functions (e.g., AWS Lambda, Google Cloud Functions, or Azure Functions). It ensures that API calls are routed correctly to the appropriate serverless function, while also handling various common concerns like security, traffic management, and load balancing.

What Is an API Gateway? An API Gateway is a server that acts as an intermediary between the client and microservices in a distributed system. It manages requests by routing them to the correct microservices, performing necessary transformations, and sending the response back to the client. In serverless architectures, the API Gateway handles HTTP requests and then triggers the appropriate serverless function to perform the required business logic.

Key responsibilities of an API Gateway in serverless systems include:

- **Request Routing**: API Gateways route requests from clients to the appropriate serverless function based on the URL path, HTTP method, or other request metadata.
- **Traffic Management**: The API Gateway helps manage and control traffic by setting rate limits, quotas, and throttling policies to protect backend services from overload.
- **Authentication and Authorization**: API Gateways can integrate with authentication mechanisms like OAuth, JWT (JSON Web Tokens), and API keys to ensure that only authorized users can access certain services.
- **Response Transformation**: The API Gateway can transform the responses from serverless functions into the desired format for the client (e.g., JSON, XML).
- **Error Handling**: It can standardize error responses and manage retries or fallbacks for failed requests.

Popular API Gateways for Serverless Architectures

1. **AWS API Gateway**: AWS API Gateway is one of the most widely used tools for managing serverless APIs. It integrates seamlessly with AWS Lambda and other AWS services, allowing developers to easily create and deploy APIs for serverless applications. API Gateway provides powerful features such as throttling, rate-limiting, and caching to improve performance and security.
    - **Benefits**: Fully managed, highly scalable, integrates with AWS Lambda and other AWS services, offers built-in authorization via AWS Cognito, and supports both RESTful and WebSocket APIs.
2. **Google Cloud Endpoints**: Google Cloud Endpoints is a fully managed API Gateway that integrates with Google Cloud Functions and other Google Cloud services. It provides tools for designing, deploying, and managing APIs with built-in features for request routing, monitoring, and security.

- ○ **Benefits**: Tight integration with Google Cloud services, support for RESTful APIs, built-in authorization and security features.
3. **Azure API Management**: Azure API Management is a fully managed API Gateway service for API consumption in Azure, providing a comprehensive solution for managing APIs, including creation, deployment, monitoring, and scaling. It integrates seamlessly with Azure Functions, providing an easy way to expose serverless functions via HTTP endpoints.
   - ○ **Benefits**: Integration with Azure Functions, API analytics and monitoring, customizable policies for security, traffic management, and caching.
4. **Kong**: Kong is an open-source API Gateway that supports both on-premises and cloud-based deployments. It's known for its scalability and flexibility and is often used in microservices and serverless architectures to route requests to serverless functions.
   - ○ **Benefits**: Open-source, supports both cloud and on-premises deployments, extensive plugin ecosystem, can be customized to fit various use cases.

By using an API Gateway in serverless systems, developers can focus on writing business logic while the Gateway takes care of the infrastructure complexities, allowing for cleaner, more maintainable code.

2.5 Serverless Databases and Storage Solutions

In a serverless architecture, managing and storing data is a crucial aspect. Serverless applications demand storage solutions that are not only scalable but also flexible, easily integrated with serverless functions, and capable of handling variable workloads with minimal overhead. Serverless databases and storage solutions address these needs by providing automatic scaling, pay-as-you-go pricing models, and seamless integration with cloud services.

1. Serverless Databases

A **serverless database** is one that automatically scales to accommodate fluctuating workloads and only charges for the storage and compute resources consumed, without the need for manual provisioning. Serverless databases are ideal for applications with unpredictable traffic or varying workloads, making them a perfect fit for serverless microservices.

- **Amazon Aurora Serverless**: Amazon Aurora Serverless is an on-demand, auto-scaling relational database service that is compatible with MySQL and PostgreSQL. It automatically adjusts its compute capacity based on application demand and pauses during inactivity to save costs. Developers don't need to manually manage the database's instance size, as Aurora Serverless handles this automatically.
    - **Use Cases**: Web and mobile applications with unpredictable or infrequent database access, startups, and low-to-medium traffic applications.
- **Google Cloud Firestore**: Google Cloud Firestore is a fully managed NoSQL document database that scales automatically to meet demand. It offers real-time synchronization and offline capabilities, making it ideal for mobile apps, web apps, and IoT applications. Firestore's serverless nature ensures that it scales seamlessly as traffic increases.
    - **Use Cases**: Real-time applications, chat systems, e-commerce apps, and applications requiring high availability.
- **Azure Cosmos DB**: Azure Cosmos DB is a globally distributed NoSQL database that supports multiple data models, including document, key-value, graph, and column-family. It's a fully managed service with automatic scaling, global distribution, and multiple consistency models. It integrates seamlessly with Azure Functions, making it ideal for serverless applications that need high availability and low latency.
    - **Use Cases**: IoT applications, global-scale applications, e-commerce platforms, and mobile apps.

25

2. Serverless Storage Solutions

Storage in serverless systems involves handling data storage and retrieval for things like user uploads, logs, and static assets. Serverless storage solutions offer scalability and cost-efficiency, particularly for use cases where large amounts of unstructured data are handled.

- **Amazon S3 (Simple Storage Service)**: AWS S3 is an object storage service that automatically scales based on demand. It's commonly used for storing large amounts of unstructured data such as images, videos, backups, and logs. Serverless functions, like AWS Lambda, can be triggered by changes to objects in S3, enabling workflows such as file processing and data transformation.
  - **Use Cases**: File storage for websites, data lakes, backup and restore, content delivery, and media storage.
- **Google Cloud Storage**: Google Cloud Storage provides a highly scalable, durable object storage solution that integrates well with Google Cloud Functions and other serverless services. It offers the same pay-as-you-go pricing model as other serverless services and is optimized for high-performance data access and storage.
  - **Use Cases**: Large-scale media storage, archiving, big data analytics, and backups.
- **Azure Blob Storage**: Azure Blob Storage is another scalable object storage solution that integrates with Azure Functions. It's ideal for storing unstructured data, such as documents, images, and logs. Like other serverless storage solutions, Azure Blob Storage scales automatically based on demand, providing a pay-per-use pricing model.
  - **Use Cases**: Storing large amounts of unstructured data, media files, logs, and backups.

3. Benefits of Serverless Databases and Storage Solutions:

- **Automatic Scaling**: These solutions automatically scale based on traffic or workload without manual intervention.
- **Cost Efficiency**: You only pay for what you use, eliminating the need for over-provisioning resources.
- **Seamless Integration**: Serverless databases and storage solutions integrate easily with serverless functions (e.g., AWS Lambda, Google Cloud Functions, and Azure Functions) for real-time data processing.
- **Reduced Operational Overhead**: No need to manage servers, handle scaling, or maintain infrastructure; the cloud provider manages it all.

Serverless databases and storage solutions significantly simplify the process of managing data and provide scalability, security, and flexibility, making them a perfect fit for serverless microservices architectures.

2.6 Authentication and Security in Serverless Architectures

When building serverless microservices, ensuring the security of applications and user data is paramount. While serverless architectures abstract much of the infrastructure management, they still require strong security measures to protect APIs, data, and sensitive information. This chapter focuses on common approaches to authentication and security within serverless systems.

1. Authentication in Serverless Architectures

Authentication refers to verifying the identity of users or systems that are attempting to access resources. In serverless applications, authentication typically involves integrating with identity management services to ensure that only authorized users can access specific resources.

- **AWS Cognito**: AWS Cognito is a popular service for implementing authentication and user management in serverless architectures. It provides features like user registration, login, and multi-factor authentication (MFA). AWS Cognito integrates seamlessly with AWS Lambda, allowing you to authenticate users and invoke serverless functions based on user roles or permissions.

- **OAuth and OpenID Connect**: OAuth is a widely adopted standard for access delegation, and OpenID Connect is an identity layer on top of OAuth that allows for authentication. These standards can be integrated into serverless applications to allow users to sign in using third-party authentication providers like Google, Facebook, or GitHub. Using OAuth and OpenID Connect, you can manage permissions and roles for users accessing your serverless APIs.
- **JWT (JSON Web Tokens)**: JWT is a compact, URL-safe token format used for securely transmitting information between parties. In serverless applications, JWT is commonly used for stateless authentication. After a user logs in, the system issues a JWT that can be passed in API requests to verify the user's identity and permissions.

2. Security in Serverless Architectures

Security in serverless systems is focused on protecting data, managing access control, securing communication channels, and monitoring threats. Some best practices for securing serverless applications include:

- **Use of Role-Based Access Control (RBAC)**: Role-based access control is essential for managing permissions in serverless environments. You can define roles for users or services and control access to serverless functions, APIs, and databases based on these roles. AWS IAM (Identity and Access Management) allows you to assign granular permissions to serverless functions.
- **Secure Communication**: Always use HTTPS (SSL/TLS encryption) to secure data transmitted between clients and serverless APIs. This ensures that sensitive data is encrypted during transmission, preventing man-in-the-middle attacks. In

addition, make sure that inter-service communication between serverless functions and other resources, such as databases or APIs, is also encrypted.

- **API Gateway Security**: As discussed earlier, API Gateways act as the entry point to serverless applications. To ensure secure access to the serverless APIs, API Gateways should be configured with security mechanisms such as rate limiting, IP whitelisting, and API keys. Additionally, integrate with identity providers like AWS Cognito or OAuth services to authenticate users.

- **Least Privilege Principle**: Apply the principle of least privilege when assigning permissions. Ensure that each serverless function or service has only the permissions necessary to perform its task, limiting the potential damage from a security breach.

- **Monitoring and Threat Detection**: Regularly monitor serverless applications for unusual behavior or potential threats. Use cloud-native security tools such as AWS CloudTrail, Azure Security Center, and Google Cloud Security Command Center to monitor access logs, detect anomalies, and receive alerts about potential security issues.

2.7 Monitoring and Observability in Serverless Environments

In serverless environments, maintaining visibility into application performance, user activity, and system health can be challenging. Without traditional servers, it can be difficult to track the execution of functions, debug issues, or monitor the health of the application. Monitoring and observability are critical to ensuring that serverless systems perform as expected and that issues can be quickly identified and resolved.

1. Monitoring in Serverless Systems

Monitoring refers to the practice of tracking system metrics such as response times, error rates, and resource utilization. In serverless systems, monitoring typically involves tracking the performance of individual serverless functions as well as the overall health of the application.

- **AWS CloudWatch**: AWS CloudWatch is a powerful monitoring service that allows you to track the performance of AWS Lambda functions, API Gateway endpoints, and other AWS services. CloudWatch collects logs, metrics, and events in real time, providing insights into the performance of serverless functions. CloudWatch Alarms can trigger actions (such as sending notifications) based on predefined thresholds, enabling proactive monitoring.

- **Google Cloud Monitoring**: Google Cloud Monitoring offers robust observability features for serverless applications. It can track key metrics like function invocations, execution time, and error rates. It integrates with Google Cloud Logging to provide comprehensive insights into the application's health and performance.

- **Azure Monitor**: Azure Monitor provides end-to-end monitoring for Azure Functions, APIs, and other services in the Azure ecosystem. It collects and analyzes telemetry data to provide insights into system performance, and it integrates with Azure Log Analytics to provide deep insights into serverless applications.

2. Observability in Serverless Systems

Observability refers to the ability to understand what is happening inside your system by collecting logs, metrics, and traces. For serverless applications, observability is essential for diagnosing issues, identifying performance bottlenecks, and ensuring that the system is operating as expected.

- **Distributed Tracing**: Distributed tracing allows you to trace a request as it moves through multiple serverless functions and services. This is particularly useful in microservices and serverless architectures, where requests may trigger a chain of events across several functions. Tools like AWS X-Ray, Google Cloud Trace, and Azure Application Insights enable distributed tracing in serverless systems.

- **Centralized Logging**: Serverless functions often produce logs that are critical for debugging and troubleshooting. Using a centralized logging service like AWS CloudWatch Logs, Google Cloud Logging, or Azure Log Analytics helps consolidate logs from different services, making it easier to search for specific events or errors.

3. Key Metrics to Track in Serverless Systems

- **Invocation Count**: The number of times a serverless function is called.
- **Execution Time**: How long a function takes to execute.
- **Error Rate**: The percentage of failed invocations.
- **Throttling**: The number of times a request is throttled due to rate-limiting.
- **Cold Starts**: The time it takes to initialize a serverless function when it's invoked after being idle.

By integrating robust monitoring and observability tools into serverless systems, developers can ensure that their applications run smoothly, troubleshoot effectively, and proactively address performance issues before they affect users.

Chapter 3: Microservices Design Patterns Overview

3.1 What Are Design Patterns?

In the context of software development, **design patterns** are general reusable solutions to common problems encountered during software design. These patterns represent best practices and proven approaches to solving design challenges in a way that ensures efficiency, maintainability, and scalability. They are typically language-independent and can be applied across different types of systems.

A design pattern is not a finished solution but rather a template that developers can adapt to solve a specific problem in their application. It provides a shared vocabulary for developers to discuss and solve common issues without reinventing the wheel each time.

Design patterns were first popularized by the book "Design Patterns: Elements of Reusable Object-Oriented Software" by Erich Gamma, Richard Helm, Ralph Johnson, and John Vlissides (often referred to as the "Gang of Four" or GoF). While these patterns originated in object-oriented programming (OOP), many of the patterns have been adapted for use in other programming paradigms, including microservices and serverless computing.

Design patterns are categorized into several types, and they focus on different aspects of the design process, such as creation, structure, and behavior. They help developers create systems that are more modular, easier to maintain, and easier to extend. They also provide a way to standardize solutions across teams, improving collaboration and reducing misunderstandings.

In microservices architectures, design patterns are particularly valuable because they help manage the complexity of building distributed systems. As applications grow and evolve, applying design patterns helps ensure that microservices work together in a cohesive and scalable way.

3.2 Types of Design Patterns in Microservices

When working with microservices, several types of design patterns are commonly applied to solve challenges related to system communication, scalability, resilience, and maintainability. These patterns help developers address common issues like inter-service communication, fault tolerance, data consistency, and security. Below are the main types of design patterns used in microservices architectures:

1. **Service Discovery Pattern** In a microservices architecture, services must often communicate with one another. However, since microservices are distributed and can scale dynamically, it can be difficult to track the network locations (IP addresses and ports) of each service. The Service Discovery pattern addresses this issue by automatically registering services and providing a mechanism for other services to discover and communicate with them.
   - **How It Works**: A service registry keeps track of the available instances of each service. When a new instance of a service is deployed, it registers itself with the registry. Other services that need to interact with that service query the registry to discover the available instances.
   - **Common Implementations**: Netflix Eureka, Consul, and Kubernetes' internal service discovery.

2. **API Gateway Pattern** The API Gateway pattern is used to provide a single entry point for all client requests in a microservices architecture. Instead of directly calling individual services, the client communicates with an API Gateway, which then routes the requests to the appropriate service. This pattern helps decouple clients from services, reducing complexity.
   - **How It Works**: The API Gateway acts as a reverse proxy, handling requests, load balancing, authentication, authorization, and response transformation. It can also provide caching, rate limiting, and monitoring for all incoming requests.
   - **Common Implementations**: AWS API Gateway, Kong, and NGINX.

33

3. **Database per Service Pattern** In a microservices architecture, each service often has its own database, ensuring that services remain loosely coupled and independent. This pattern addresses the need to maintain data consistency in a decentralized manner by assigning each microservice its own database, typically with its own schema.
   - **How It Works**: Each microservice manages its own database, and no service has direct access to another service's database. Services communicate through APIs to exchange data and maintain consistency.
   - **Benefits**: This pattern helps ensure data isolation, resilience, and scalability, but it can also introduce challenges in maintaining data consistency and synchronization between services.
4. **Event Sourcing Pattern** The Event Sourcing pattern is used to capture every change to an application's state as an event, rather than storing just the final state. This approach enables the application to rebuild its state by replaying events in order. It is particularly useful in scenarios where tracking state changes and ensuring consistency across distributed systems is crucial.
   - **How It Works**: Every update to a service's state is captured as an event and stored in an event store. These events can be processed by other services or used to reconstruct the state of the service at any given point in time.
   - **Benefits**: Event sourcing enables event-driven systems and provides an audit trail of changes to the system, making it useful for systems requiring high availability and durability.
   - **Common Implementations**: Kafka, RabbitMQ, and EventStore.
5. **CQRS (Command Query Responsibility Segregation) Pattern** CQRS separates the operations that modify data (commands) from those that read data (queries). This pattern is useful in scenarios where read and write operations have significantly different requirements in terms of performance and scalability. By using separate models for reading and writing data, CQRS allows services to be optimized for their specific roles.

- **How It Works**: The command side handles operations that change the state of the system (e.g., creating or updating data), while the query side handles read operations. In some implementations, the read side may be optimized using read replicas or caching to improve performance.
- **Benefits**: This pattern improves scalability and performance by separating read and write workloads, but it can introduce complexity in maintaining data consistency between the two models.
- **Common Implementations**: Axon Framework, EventStore, and Spring Cloud.

6. **Saga Pattern** The Saga pattern addresses the problem of managing long-running, distributed transactions in microservices. In traditional monolithic architectures, transactions are typically managed by a relational database with ACID (Atomicity, Consistency, Isolation, Durability) properties. However, microservices require a different approach since each service often has its own database and may be deployed in different locations.

- **How It Works**: Instead of using a centralized database for a distributed transaction, the Saga pattern splits the transaction into a series of smaller, isolated transactions that are executed across multiple services. Each step in the saga is coordinated using messages, and if one step fails, compensating transactions are used to revert the changes made by previous steps.
- **Benefits**: The Saga pattern ensures that microservices can handle distributed transactions reliably, but it introduces complexity in coordinating and managing failure scenarios.
- **Common Implementations**: Camunda, NServiceBus, and Axon Framework.

7. **Sidecar Pattern** The Sidecar pattern is used to manage auxiliary functions that are closely related to the main service but are isolated in a separate process. This pattern is often used for cross-cutting concerns like logging, monitoring, or

security, allowing these services to be deployed independently of the main application logic.

- ○ **How It Works**: A sidecar is deployed alongside the main service, often as a separate container or process. It shares the same network space and can interact with the main service, but it is decoupled and manages its own lifecycle.
- ○ **Benefits**: The Sidecar pattern enables the main service to remain focused on business logic, while the sidecar handles additional responsibilities like configuration management, security, and telemetry.
- ○ **Common Implementations**: Istio, Envoy Proxy, and Linkerd.

8. **Strangler Fig Pattern** The Strangler Fig pattern is often used when migrating from a monolithic system to a microservices architecture. It involves gradually replacing parts of the monolithic system with microservices, eventually "strangling" the monolith as microservices take over its functionality.

- ○ **How It Works**: New functionality is developed as microservices, while the legacy system continues to handle existing functionality. Over time, the microservices incrementally replace the monolith, until the old system is no longer needed.
- ○ **Benefits**: This pattern allows for gradual migration without requiring a complete rewrite of the system, reducing risk and enabling the team to continue delivering value while transitioning to a microservices architecture.

3.3 The Role of Design Patterns in Serverless Architectures

Design patterns are just as essential in serverless architectures as they are in traditional architectures, especially given the unique characteristics and challenges of serverless computing. While serverless computing abstracts away infrastructure management and provides automatic scaling, it also introduces new complexities related to distributed systems, state management, event handling, and fault tolerance.

Design patterns in serverless architectures help developers solve these challenges in a scalable, maintainable, and efficient way. Below are some key roles that design patterns play in serverless environments:

1. **Handling Asynchronous Communication**: Serverless functions are often used in event-driven systems, where services need to communicate asynchronously through events. Design patterns such as the **Event Sourcing Pattern** and the **Saga Pattern** are crucial in serverless systems to ensure that events are processed and that transactions across distributed functions are handled reliably. These patterns allow for the seamless communication and management of state across multiple serverless functions.

2. **Ensuring Resilience and Fault Tolerance**: One of the main challenges of building serverless applications is ensuring that the system remains resilient even in the face of failures. Patterns like the **Circuit Breaker Pattern** and **Retry Pattern** help manage errors by preventing cascading failures, retrying failed requests, and isolating issues before they affect the entire system. Serverless functions often involve network communication, so having resilience mechanisms in place is critical for maintaining availability.

3. **Managing Service Communication**: While serverless functions are highly decoupled, they still need to communicate with other services. The **API Gateway Pattern** and **Sidecar Pattern** are particularly useful in serverless architectures, as they help manage external communication, ensure proper routing, and handle cross-cutting concerns such as logging, security, and monitoring.

4. **Scaling with Demand**: Serverless architectures are inherently scalable, but without the right patterns, applications may struggle with scaling efficiently. Design patterns like the **Bulkhead Pattern** and **Throttling Pattern** help ensure that serverless applications can handle varying levels of load and that individual services do not become overwhelmed during traffic spikes.

5. **Managing State in Stateless Environments**: Serverless functions are typically stateless, but many applications require state management to function properly. Design patterns such as **CQRS** and **Event Sourcing** are used in serverless systems to separate read and write operations, manage state changes through events, and ensure eventual consistency across distributed services.

By applying these design patterns, developers can build serverless applications that are not only scalable and resilient but also easier to maintain, extend, and integrate with other services. Serverless design patterns ensure that serverless applications can operate effectively while handling the challenges of distributed computing, asynchronous communication, and dynamic scaling.

3.4 Benefits of Applying Design Patterns in Serverless

Applying design patterns to serverless architectures offers numerous benefits that can significantly enhance the performance, scalability, and maintainability of applications. These patterns not only provide a systematic way to address common challenges but also promote consistency and efficiency across the development process. Below are some key benefits of using design patterns in serverless environments:

1. **Improved Scalability and Performance**
   One of the main reasons to apply design patterns in serverless architectures is to effectively scale applications based on demand. Serverless platforms like AWS Lambda, Google Cloud Functions, and Azure Functions automatically scale functions based on incoming events. However, without proper patterns, serverless applications may face issues like excessive resource consumption, inefficient scaling, or bottlenecks.
   Design patterns such as the **Bulkhead Pattern** and **Throttling Pattern** help optimize resource usage by ensuring that services are isolated and traffic is managed effectively. These patterns help prevent overloads in specific services

and ensure that other parts of the system continue functioning smoothly even under high traffic conditions.

2. **Fault Isolation and Resilience**

   Serverless environments, like all distributed systems, can be prone to failures. While serverless platforms often provide some level of fault tolerance, implementing resilience patterns can help prevent cascading failures and improve system availability.

   Patterns like the **Circuit Breaker Pattern** and **Retry Pattern** help identify and mitigate issues before they affect the entire system. These patterns detect failures in individual functions, prevent the system from overloading with failed requests, and allow automatic retries or fallback operations, ensuring higher availability and better fault isolation.

3. **Cost Efficiency**

   One of the major advantages of serverless computing is its pay-as-you-go pricing model, where you only pay for the execution time of your functions. However, without proper design, serverless applications could result in unnecessary costs due to inefficient resource usage.

   By applying patterns like **Event Sourcing** and **CQRS**, developers can optimize how data is read and written, improving both cost and performance.

   Event-driven patterns like **Event Sourcing** allow applications to store only essential events, reducing the need for expensive database operations and storage. Similarly, **CQRS** can optimize read and write operations separately, ensuring that resources are used efficiently.

4. **Simplified Maintenance and Updates**

   Maintaining a serverless application can be challenging, especially as the number of functions grows. Design patterns help by simplifying the architecture and making it more modular.

   By applying patterns such as the **Database per Service Pattern** or **API Gateway Pattern**, you can break down services into smaller, independently deployable units. This modularity makes it easier to update or modify individual components without affecting the entire system. Furthermore, by applying **Event Sourcing**, you create an immutable log of state changes, which can help developers easily troubleshoot issues and maintain consistency across services.

5. **Enhanced Security**

Security is critical in any architecture, but it can be particularly challenging in serverless environments due to the distributed nature of the system. Applying design patterns like **Role-Based Access Control (RBAC)** and **API Gateway Security** ensures that only authorized services and users can interact with specific functions or data.

Using an **API Gateway** as the entry point into the system centralizes security concerns, enabling authentication, authorization, and access control policies to be implemented in one place. Additionally, **RBAC** helps enforce granular access controls by allowing developers to define roles and permissions for different services, ensuring that only those who need access to sensitive resources can get it.

6. **Better Communication and Data Flow Management**

In a microservices-based system, efficient communication between services is key. Serverless systems often rely on asynchronous communication to trigger functions in response to events. Without a clear strategy for managing communication, services may become disorganized, leading to delays and failures.

The **API Gateway Pattern**, **Event Sourcing**, and **Message Queue Patterns** are designed to help ensure that communication is structured and managed properly. They allow different services to communicate efficiently, maintain data consistency, and decouple different parts of the system, making the architecture more resilient and easier to scale.

7. **Faster Development and Iteration**

Design patterns also provide a standardized way of solving problems, allowing developers to avoid reinventing the wheel each time they face a challenge. By using well-established patterns, developers can implement features faster, reduce development time, and minimize errors.

For example, patterns like **CQRS** enable the separation of read and write models, making it easier to evolve the system and scale parts of the application independently. This leads to faster iteration and development cycles, which is crucial in today's fast-moving tech environment.

3.5 Challenges When Implementing Design Patterns in Serverless Environments

While applying design patterns in serverless architectures offers numerous advantages, there are also several challenges developers must consider when implementing these patterns. These challenges primarily stem from the inherent characteristics of serverless computing, such as the stateless nature of serverless functions, the complexity of managing distributed systems, and the need for high availability.

1. **State Management**

   Serverless functions are inherently stateless, meaning they don't retain any information between invocations. While this is an advantage in terms of scaling and fault tolerance, it can make certain design patterns, such as **Event Sourcing** or **CQRS**, more difficult to implement.

   Maintaining state in serverless environments often requires external systems, such as databases, event stores, or caches, which can add complexity and overhead. For instance, implementing **CQRS** means managing two separate data models—one for reading and one for writing—which can be cumbersome in a stateless environment where both models must be consistently synchronized.

2. **Cold Starts and Latency**

   One of the most significant challenges in serverless computing is the **cold start** phenomenon, where functions experience a delay when they are invoked for the first time after being idle. Cold starts can introduce latency in serverless applications, especially for real-time systems.

   While design patterns like the **Retry Pattern** can mitigate the effects of cold starts by automatically retrying failed requests, they cannot eliminate the latency altogether. Developers need to design serverless applications to minimize cold start impact, which may involve optimizing the code or reducing function complexity.

3. **Complexity of Distributed Systems**

   Microservices and serverless architectures often result in highly distributed systems, which can be challenging to manage and monitor. Design patterns like **Event Sourcing**, **Saga**, and **CQRS** help address the complexity of managing distributed data and transactions, but they also introduce their own challenges. For example, with **Saga Pattern**, you need to ensure that transactions across multiple services are coordinated correctly, which may involve implementing complex orchestration logic. This can lead to difficulties in ensuring data consistency, handling failures, and managing event flows across distributed components.

4. **Vendor Lock-In**

   Serverless computing platforms, such as AWS Lambda, Google Cloud Functions, and Azure Functions, often come with vendor-specific tools and services. This can lead to **vendor lock-in**, where the application becomes tightly coupled to a specific cloud provider, making it difficult to migrate to another provider without significant changes to the system.

   Design patterns like **API Gateway** and **Service Discovery** can help reduce vendor lock-in by abstracting communication between services and providing flexibility in how services interact. However, for some patterns, such as **Event Sourcing**, relying on cloud-specific services for event storage and management may limit portability.

5. **Monitoring and Debugging**

   Monitoring and debugging serverless applications can be challenging because serverless functions are typically distributed across multiple services and triggered by a variety of events. This complexity can make it difficult to trace errors, monitor performance, and gather detailed logs.

Implementing design patterns like **Event Sourcing** or **Saga** can further complicate debugging because events and transactions are distributed across multiple services. Developers must leverage monitoring tools and practices like distributed tracing, centralized logging, and performance tracking to gain visibility into serverless systems.

6. **Overhead of Maintaining Multiple Patterns**

   While design patterns provide structure and consistency, they can also introduce overhead in terms of complexity. For example, applying multiple patterns such as **Event Sourcing**, **CQRS**, and **Saga** in a serverless application can lead to a highly complex architecture that may be difficult to maintain, especially as the application scales.

   Developers need to carefully assess whether the benefits of implementing multiple patterns outweigh the added complexity. In some cases, it may be more practical to implement simpler patterns that solve specific problems rather than trying to apply multiple patterns that complicate the system unnecessarily.

3.6 How to Choose the Right Design Pattern

Choosing the right design pattern for a serverless microservices architecture requires careful consideration of the application's specific needs, goals, and constraints. Below are several factors to help guide the decision-making process when selecting a design pattern:

1. **Nature of the Application** Consider the primary requirements of the application. Does it need to handle high volumes of real-time data? Is it a read-heavy application that requires optimized query performance? Understanding the application's specific requirements will help you select the most suitable design pattern.
   - ○ **For real-time, event-driven applications**, patterns like **Event Sourcing** and **CQRS** are great choices because they allow the system to react to events as they occur, processing data asynchronously.

- For applications with complex transactions, the Saga Pattern is ideal for managing distributed transactions while maintaining data consistency.

2. Scalability Requirements If the application needs to handle large traffic volumes or scale dynamically, patterns like Bulkhead and Throttling can be applied to ensure that the system can scale effectively without becoming overloaded.
    - Bulkhead ensures that failures in one part of the system do not affect others, while Throttling helps manage traffic to prevent overloads. These patterns are particularly useful when scaling serverless functions, as they help manage resource consumption and maintain responsiveness.

3. Data Consistency and State Management Serverless architectures often involve services that need to access and manipulate data. When choosing design patterns, consider whether the application requires strong data consistency or if eventual consistency is acceptable.
    - For applications requiring strict consistency, patterns like Event Sourcing and CQRS can help ensure that data is correctly updated and managed across different services.
    - For applications that can tolerate eventual consistency, simpler patterns like API Gateway or Database per Service may be more appropriate.

4. Complexity vs. Simplicity While design patterns provide valuable solutions, they can also add complexity to the system. If the application is relatively simple, it may not require the full range of advanced patterns. Opting for simpler patterns can help avoid unnecessary complexity.
    - For simple applications or services, a pattern like API Gateway for routing requests and basic Database per Service for isolation might be sufficient. These patterns are easy to implement and maintain while still providing a good level of separation and scalability.

5. Monitoring and Debugging Needs Monitoring and debugging are critical for maintaining serverless applications. If complex event flows and distributed

transactions are involved, choosing patterns that provide clear visibility and traceability is essential.

- If you need to track the state of an application across services, **Event Sourcing** or **Saga** can help by providing an audit trail. However, they also require robust monitoring systems to trace events across multiple services.

6. **Team Expertise and Familiarity** Finally, consider the experience and familiarity of your development team with different design patterns. Some patterns, like **Event Sourcing** or **CQRS**, require a deeper understanding of event-driven architecture and distributed systems. If your team lacks experience with these patterns, it might be worthwhile to start with simpler patterns and gradually introduce more advanced ones as needed.

By carefully evaluating the specific needs of your application and the expertise of your team, you can choose the right design patterns that strike a balance between complexity, scalability, performance, and maintainability. This ensures that the serverless microservices architecture will be efficient, resilient, and easier to manage over time.

Chapter 4: Core Microservices Design Patterns for Serverless Applications

4.1 The Decomposition Pattern: Breaking Down Large Systems

In the world of microservices, **decomposition** is one of the foundational design patterns. The **Decomposition Pattern** is the process of breaking down a large, monolithic application into smaller, independent, and loosely coupled microservices. Each microservice is responsible for a specific piece of the application's functionality, and can be developed, deployed, and scaled independently. This is particularly important in serverless architectures where scalability, isolation, and independent updates are critical.

What Is the Decomposition Pattern? Decomposition involves breaking down a large and complex application into smaller, manageable services that each focus on a distinct business capability or function. This allows for easier development, testing, and deployment, as well as enhanced flexibility and scalability.

In traditional monolithic applications, all the features and components of the application are tightly coupled and reside within a single codebase. This leads to challenges as the application grows larger, such as difficulty in scaling, slower deployments, and the potential for one component failure to affect the entire system.

By applying the Decomposition Pattern in serverless systems, these issues are mitigated. Serverless platforms like AWS Lambda, Google Cloud Functions, and Azure Functions naturally align with microservices architectures by enabling developers to deploy small, isolated functions that respond to specific events.

Key Benefits of the Decomposition Pattern in Serverless Systems:

1. **Improved Scalability:**
   Microservices are often stateless and independently scalable. When each service is isolated, it can be scaled up or down based on demand, which is particularly

valuable in serverless environments where functions automatically scale depending on the number of incoming requests. For example, a service handling user authentication can be scaled independently from a service that processes payments, optimizing resource usage.

2. **Faster Development and Deployment:**

   Microservices can be developed, tested, and deployed independently of one another. With serverless computing, the deployment process becomes even faster because each function or service only involves deploying a small piece of code rather than the entire system. As a result, developers can quickly iterate and release features without waiting for other parts of the application to be ready.

3. **Fault Isolation:**

   One of the key advantages of microservices is the ability to isolate faults. If a particular service encounters an issue, it doesn't bring down the entire system. Serverless functions, in particular, are designed to handle failures gracefully by automatically retrying or invoking fallback logic. This reduces the risk of large-scale failures in the system.

4. **Technology Agnostic:**

   Decomposition allows for different microservices to be developed using different technologies. For example, one service might be written in Python to handle data processing, while another could be in JavaScript for handling web requests. This flexibility allows development teams to use the best tool for each job, optimizing performance and resource use.

5. **Simplified Maintenance:**

   Since each microservice is independently deployable and isolated, updates to one service do not impact others. Serverless environments, where functions are triggered by events, further streamline this process. For example, a database update function can be modified or updated independently from a function that processes incoming HTTP requests.

Challenges with Decomposition: While decomposition offers significant benefits, it also introduces some complexities. One challenge is managing the communication between microservices, as well as ensuring that data consistency is maintained. Serverless functions need to be carefully designed to ensure that inter-service communication is efficient and reliable, using patterns like **Event-Driven Architecture** or **API Gateway** to manage requests and responses.

Another challenge is ensuring that services remain loosely coupled but still have consistent interfaces for interaction. This requires careful consideration of APIs, data formats, and versioning to avoid issues as services evolve over time.

4.2 The Database per Service Pattern: Ensuring Data Isolation

One of the core challenges in microservices architecture is managing data consistency and ensuring that each service has the appropriate level of autonomy. The **Database per Service Pattern** addresses this challenge by ensuring that each microservice has its own dedicated database. This promotes **data isolation** between services, preventing one service from directly manipulating or accessing the database of another service.

What Is the Database per Service Pattern? In a microservices architecture, each service is responsible for its own business logic, and ideally, it should also own its data. The **Database per Service Pattern** stipulates that each microservice maintains its own database, which could be a relational database, NoSQL database, or any other form of persistent storage.

This pattern contrasts with traditional monolithic applications, where a single database is used by the entire application. By using the Database per Service Pattern, each microservice becomes more independent and isolated, which supports modularity and scalability.

Key Benefits of the Database per Service Pattern in Serverless Systems:

1. **Data Ownership and Autonomy:**

   By giving each microservice its own database, it becomes the sole owner of its data. This autonomy allows each service to choose the best database solution based on its requirements, whether that's a NoSQL database for high throughput or a relational database for complex queries. For serverless applications, this autonomy ensures that services remain decoupled and can scale independently.

2. **Improved Performance:**

   Because each service has its own database, there is no need to share resources with other services. This can lead to better performance, as each service is optimized for its specific data access needs. Additionally, by using separate databases, it's easier to scale specific parts of the application based on demand.

3. **Fault Isolation:**

   One of the key advantages of this pattern is that it helps isolate faults. If one service's database becomes unavailable or encounters an issue, other services are unaffected. Serverless functions that rely on these databases can be independently scaled and can be designed to handle failures gracefully through retries or fallback strategies.

4. **Easier Data Management and Governance:**

   Each service has control over its database, making it easier to enforce data access policies, security measures, and data privacy. Serverless architectures often require managing multiple instances of databases across different services, and the **Database per Service Pattern** provides a clear separation of responsibilities, making it easier to implement governance and compliance standards.

Challenges with the Database per Service Pattern: While the **Database per Service Pattern** provides significant benefits, it also introduces challenges related to maintaining data consistency across services. In microservices architectures, data consistency can be difficult to manage, especially when services need to share data.

To maintain consistency across databases, developers need to implement strategies like **Eventual Consistency** or **Saga Patterns**, which ensure that updates to one service's data are reflected in other services over time. Additionally, coordinating queries across multiple databases can be more complex, as each database may use a different query language, schema, or storage model.

4.3 The API Gateway Pattern: Simplifying Communication

In a microservices architecture, the **API Gateway Pattern** plays a vital role in simplifying communication between clients (such as web or mobile applications) and the microservices that form the back-end of an application. The API Gateway serves as a single entry point for all incoming requests, routing them to the appropriate microservice, and performing additional tasks such as authentication, rate limiting, caching, and logging.

What Is the API Gateway Pattern? An **API Gateway** is a server that acts as an intermediary between the client and the microservices. It provides a unified API for clients to interact with multiple backend services. Instead of making direct calls to each microservice, clients communicate with the API Gateway, which then routes the requests to the correct microservice.

The API Gateway pattern is particularly useful in serverless applications, where there may be dozens or even hundreds of microservices, each responsible for different pieces of functionality. Instead of managing multiple API endpoints for each service, an API Gateway simplifies client interaction by consolidating these endpoints into a single entry point.

Key Benefits of the API Gateway Pattern in Serverless Systems:

1. **Simplified Client Interaction:**
   One of the primary benefits of using an API Gateway is that it consolidates multiple endpoints into a single entry point for clients. This reduces the

complexity of client-side code, as clients only need to interact with one URL or API endpoint, regardless of how many services exist behind the scenes.

2. **Centralized Authentication and Security:**
   The API Gateway can handle authentication and authorization for all microservices, centralizing security management. By integrating with identity management systems like **OAuth** or **JWT**, the API Gateway can ensure that only authorized users can access specific microservices.

3. **Load Balancing and Traffic Management:**
   The API Gateway acts as a reverse proxy, distributing incoming requests across the appropriate microservices. This enables load balancing and helps optimize the performance of the system by ensuring that no single service is overwhelmed by too many requests. In serverless environments, this pattern helps scale individual serverless functions based on incoming traffic.

4. **Rate Limiting and Throttling:**
   The API Gateway can enforce rate limits to protect backend services from excessive load. It can throttle requests based on predefined rules, preventing a flood of traffic from overwhelming the serverless functions. This is particularly important in serverless systems where scaling up or down may take a few seconds.

5. **Request Transformation and Aggregation:**
   An API Gateway can transform incoming requests into the format expected by the backend microservices and also aggregate responses from multiple services into a single response to send back to the client. This reduces the complexity of client requests and ensures consistent, optimized communication between the client and the backend.

6. **Centralized Monitoring and Logging:**
   The API Gateway can act as a central point for logging and monitoring all incoming requests and outgoing responses. By tracking request metrics like response time, status codes, and error rates, the API Gateway provides valuable insights into the health and performance of the microservices.

Challenges with the API Gateway Pattern: While the API Gateway Pattern provides many advantages, it can also introduce certain challenges. The API Gateway becomes a single point of failure, and if it goes down, all communication between clients and backend services is disrupted. Therefore, it's essential to ensure that the API Gateway is highly available and redundant.

Additionally, the API Gateway can become a bottleneck if not properly managed, as it has to handle all incoming traffic and routing. It also adds complexity in terms of managing the routing logic, transformation, and load balancing, particularly when the number of microservices increases.

Popular API Gateway Solutions for Serverless:

- **AWS API Gateway**: A fully managed service that enables developers to create and manage APIs for serverless applications. It integrates seamlessly with AWS Lambda and other AWS services.
- **Google Cloud Endpoints**: A fully managed API Gateway solution from Google Cloud that supports serverless functions and can be easily integrated with other Google Cloud services.
- **Azure API Management**: Microsoft's solution for managing APIs across services, including serverless applications. It provides a range of features such as security, analytics, and rate limiting.

By applying the **API Gateway Pattern**, serverless microservices architectures can be simplified, optimized, and made more secure, enhancing both the client and developer experience while maintaining high availability and flexibility.

4.4 The Event Sourcing Pattern: Managing State Changes in Serverless

In serverless and microservices architectures, managing state can be a significant challenge, especially when functions are stateless and don't persist data between invocations. The **Event Sourcing Pattern** is an architectural pattern designed to address this challenge by persisting state changes as a sequence of events, rather than just storing the current state.

What Is Event Sourcing? Event Sourcing is the practice of storing all changes to the state of an application as a sequence of immutable events. Instead of saving only the latest state of an entity in a database, every state change is recorded as an event. This allows developers to reconstruct the full history of an entity's state by replaying the events in order.

In serverless systems, this pattern can be particularly beneficial because serverless functions are stateless by design. Storing state in events ensures that state changes are never lost, and it allows for a more reliable and transparent system that can be audited and debugged more easily.

Key Benefits of the Event Sourcing Pattern in Serverless Systems:

1. **Full History of Changes**: By recording every change as an event, Event Sourcing provides a complete and accurate history of an entity's state. This can be useful for auditing, troubleshooting, or debugging, as you can replay events to track how the state has evolved over time.

2. **Event Replay**: If the state of a service or function is ever lost or corrupted, the events can be replayed from the event store to reconstruct the current state. This provides resilience and fault tolerance, which is essential in serverless applications where state persistence can be challenging.

3. **Scalability**: Event Sourcing works well in highly scalable environments, especially when combined with event-driven architectures. Serverless functions can process events asynchronously, enabling the system to handle large volumes of data or events at scale. For example, event stores like AWS Kinesis or Google Cloud Pub/Sub can handle high-throughput data streams, ensuring that events are processed reliably.

4. **Decoupling and Flexibility**: The Event Sourcing pattern enables services to be loosely coupled because each service can process events at its own pace, without

being dependent on the state of other services. This allows for greater flexibility and easier scaling of individual services without worrying about direct dependencies.

5. **Enhanced Integration with Other Services**: In serverless architectures, Event Sourcing makes it easier to integrate with other services. Events can trigger downstream processes or functions, allowing for real-time processing or communication between services. For example, an event could trigger a function that updates an external database or sends a notification to a user.

Challenges of Event Sourcing:

1. **Complexity in Managing Events**: The Event Sourcing pattern can introduce complexity in managing events, especially when dealing with large numbers of events or complex event-driven workflows. Developers must ensure that events are correctly sequenced, and that the event store can handle high-throughput data efficiently.

2. **Eventual Consistency**: Because events are processed asynchronously, Event Sourcing typically relies on eventual consistency. This can lead to challenges in ensuring that data remains consistent across different services or components in real-time, which can be especially challenging in distributed systems.

3. **Event Store Management**: Storing and managing events in an event store can require specialized infrastructure, such as dedicated storage or messaging queues, to handle the data. Ensuring the durability and availability of events becomes critical, as losing events would compromise the entire system.

4.5 The CQRS Pattern (Command Query Responsibility Segregation)

The **CQRS Pattern (Command Query Responsibility Segregation)** is a design pattern that separates the processes that modify data (commands) from those that query data (queries). It is particularly useful in applications where the read and write operations have distinct requirements and performance characteristics.

What Is CQRS? CQRS is based on the principle of separating the responsibilities of reading and writing data. In a traditional application, a single model is used for both reading and writing data. However, in CQRS, two separate models are used: one for handling **commands** (which alter data) and another for handling **queries** (which retrieve data). These models can be optimized for their specific tasks, improving performance and scalability.

In serverless environments, CQRS is particularly effective because it allows different components of the system to be independently scaled based on their specific workload. For example, the write model might need to handle high-throughput, transactional data, while the read model could focus on optimizing performance for complex queries or aggregations.

Key Benefits of the CQRS Pattern in Serverless Systems:

1. **Optimized Read and Write Operations**: By separating the read and write models, you can optimize each one for its specific requirements. The write model can be focused on handling transactions, enforcing business rules, and maintaining consistency, while the read model can be optimized for fast queries, caching, and complex aggregations.

2. **Improved Performance and Scalability**: In a traditional architecture, the read and write workloads are handled by the same database, which can become a bottleneck as the application scales. With CQRS, you can independently scale the read and write models. For example, you could scale the query side using read replicas or in-memory caching, while scaling the command side with more powerful database solutions.

3. **Separation of Concerns**: CQRS helps maintain a clear separation of concerns, allowing developers to focus on specific aspects of the application. By splitting the application's logic into two parts (commands and queries), the code becomes more modular and easier to maintain.

4. **Flexibility in Event Handling**: The CQRS pattern is often used in combination with event-driven architectures and **Event Sourcing**. When a command is executed, it generates events that can be stored, processed, and used to update the read model. This enables real-time updates and ensures that the read model remains consistent with the write model.

5. **Improved Security and Validation**: Separating the command and query sides of the application allows you to apply different security rules and validation for each. For example, write operations (commands) can require strict validation and authorization, while read operations (queries) can have more relaxed security controls.

Challenges with the CQRS Pattern:

1. **Increased Complexity**: Implementing CQRS can increase the complexity of the system, as developers must manage two different models and ensure that they remain synchronized. Maintaining consistency between the command and query sides, especially in distributed systems, can be challenging.

2. **Eventual Consistency**: As with Event Sourcing, CQRS often relies on eventual consistency. This means that the read model may not immediately reflect changes made to the write model, leading to temporary inconsistencies between the two. Managing eventual consistency requires careful design and monitoring.

3. **Infrastructure Requirements**: The CQRS pattern may require more infrastructure to handle the separate command and query models. For example, you might need different databases or services for the read and write sides, which could increase operational overhead.

4.6 The Saga Pattern: Managing Distributed Transactions

The **Saga Pattern** is used to manage long-running, distributed transactions that span multiple services in a microservices architecture. In traditional monolithic systems, transactions are typically managed using a single, centralized database with ACID

(Atomicity, Consistency, Isolation, Durability) properties. However, in distributed systems, especially those based on microservices and serverless architectures, managing transactions across multiple services is more complex.

What Is the Saga Pattern? The Saga Pattern breaks a distributed transaction into a series of smaller, independent transactions (called **saga steps**) that are executed across different services. Each step in the saga is a local transaction that can either succeed or fail. If a step fails, compensating transactions are executed to roll back the changes made by previous steps in the saga.

Sagas can be implemented in two main ways:

- **Choreography**: Each service involved in the saga is responsible for triggering the next service in the sequence.
- **Orchestration**: A central service (called the **orchestrator**) coordinates the saga by telling each service when to execute its transaction.

In serverless systems, the Saga Pattern is essential for ensuring that distributed transactions are completed successfully, even if individual functions or services fail.

Key Benefits of the Saga Pattern in Serverless Systems:

1. **Fault Tolerance**: The Saga Pattern ensures that if one part of a distributed transaction fails, the system can still maintain consistency by rolling back changes with compensating transactions. This prevents partial updates from being committed, ensuring data integrity.
2. **Distributed Transactions Management**: In a serverless architecture, different functions might need to be involved in the same transaction. The Saga Pattern helps manage these transactions across multiple services, ensuring that each function performs its part without the need for centralized transaction management.

3. **Scalability**: Sagas are highly scalable because each transaction is broken into smaller, isolated steps that can be processed independently. In serverless environments, this allows each function to be scaled independently based on demand, without needing to scale the entire transaction process.

4. **Asynchronous Processing**: The Saga Pattern fits well with serverless, event-driven architectures, where each step in the saga can be triggered by events or messages. This allows for asynchronous processing and decoupling of services, improving system resilience.

Challenges with the Saga Pattern:

1. **Complexity in Orchestration**: Managing the coordination of distributed transactions can be complex, especially in choreography-based implementations where each service must know how to trigger the next service. In orchestration, a single point of failure in the orchestrator can disrupt the entire saga.

2. **Compensating Transactions**: Implementing compensating transactions can be difficult because each service must have logic to undo changes when a transaction fails. This can be error-prone, particularly when multiple services are involved, and maintaining consistency across them can be challenging.

4.7 The Strangler Fig Pattern: Migrating from Monolithic to Microservices

The **Strangler Fig Pattern** is a popular approach to gradually migrate from a monolithic system to a microservices-based architecture. It allows organizations to replace parts of their monolithic application with microservices in a controlled, incremental manner, reducing the risk and complexity of a big-bang migration.

What Is the Strangler Fig Pattern? The Strangler Fig Pattern takes inspiration from a type of plant known for slowly overtaking its host tree, replacing it over time. In the context of software, this pattern involves replacing parts of a monolithic application with microservices, step by step. New functionality is built as microservices, and existing functionality is progressively moved from the monolith to these new services.

Key Benefits of the Strangler Fig Pattern:

1. **Incremental Migration**: The Strangler Fig Pattern enables organizations to migrate to microservices without needing to rewrite the entire monolith in one go. This allows the team to focus on smaller, manageable parts of the system and migrate them incrementally.

2. **Reduced Risk**: By incrementally replacing components, the Strangler Fig Pattern reduces the risk associated with large-scale migrations. The old system continues to operate while the new services are integrated, allowing teams to test and validate the migration in real-time.

3. **Smooth Transition**: The pattern allows for a gradual transition to microservices, where legacy functionality can be kept in place while new features are built as microservices. This avoids downtime and service disruptions, ensuring that the system remains operational throughout the migration process.

Challenges with the Strangler Fig Pattern:

1. **Complex Integration**: As parts of the monolithic application are replaced, there will be integration challenges between the old monolith and the new microservices. Ensuring that both systems work together without introducing inconsistencies or errors can be complex.

2. **Overlapping Code**: During the migration process, there may be overlapping code in the monolith and the new microservices. Managing this overlapping functionality and avoiding duplicated logic can be tricky.

4.8 The Sidecar Pattern: Enhancing Microservice Functionality

The **Sidecar Pattern** is a design pattern in which auxiliary or supporting functionality is added to a microservice by deploying a separate, closely associated service (the sidecar).

This auxiliary service runs alongside the main service, providing additional features like monitoring, logging, or security without altering the core business logic.

What Is the Sidecar Pattern? In the Sidecar Pattern, the sidecar service is deployed as a separate container or process that runs alongside the main service. The sidecar shares the same network namespace and interacts with the main service, but it is isolated in terms of its lifecycle and responsibilities.

Key Benefits of the Sidecar Pattern in Serverless Systems:

1. **Separation of Concerns**: The sidecar allows the main service to focus on business logic while the sidecar handles cross-cutting concerns like monitoring, security, or logging. This separation helps keep the core application code clean and focused.

2. **Improved Flexibility and Maintainability**: Since the sidecar is a separate service, it can be developed, deployed, and scaled independently of the main service. This makes it easier to introduce new features or functionality to the system without altering the core service logic.

3. **Enhanced Observability**: Sidecars can be used to implement logging, tracing, and monitoring for microservices, which is particularly useful in serverless systems where services are often stateless and distributed. Sidecars can also provide consistent observability features across services in a uniform manner.

4. **Cross-Cutting Features**: The Sidecar Pattern is ideal for implementing features like **security (authentication and authorization)**, **rate limiting**, **caching**, **traffic routing**, or **service discovery**, all without modifying the core business logic of the microservice.

Challenges with the Sidecar Pattern:

1. **Increased Complexity**: Introducing sidecars can increase the complexity of the system, as you now have multiple services to manage. Monitoring and debugging can become more difficult, as each service (both the main service and the sidecar) needs to be managed, deployed, and maintained.

2. **Overhead**: While sidecars provide useful functionality, they also introduce additional resource consumption and operational overhead. This is particularly true in serverless systems, where each sidecar service will need to scale with the main service, which can lead to higher costs.

By leveraging the **Sidecar Pattern**, teams can enhance the functionality and resilience of microservices without compromising the core business logic, ensuring the system is both flexible and scalable.

Chapter 5: Advanced Serverless Microservices Patterns

5.1 The Event-Driven Architecture Pattern

An **Event-Driven Architecture (EDA)** is a design pattern that promotes the decoupling of services and components by using events to trigger actions and communicate between them. In serverless microservices, EDA is especially powerful because it allows services to respond asynchronously to events without needing to tightly couple components.

What Is Event-Driven Architecture? In an Event-Driven Architecture, services are designed to react to events generated by other services or systems. An event can be any change in state or significant occurrence in the system, such as a user action, a system-generated message, or a change in data. These events trigger specific actions or processes that are defined in the system.

For example, in a serverless microservices architecture, a user submitting a form could trigger an event that calls a serverless function to process the data, and the processing of the data might trigger another event to update the database or send an email notification.

Key Benefits of the Event-Driven Architecture Pattern in Serverless Systems:

1. **Loose Coupling**: Event-driven systems decouple the components or services, meaning that producers and consumers of events don't need to know about each other's existence or implementation. This reduces inter-service dependencies, making the system more flexible and easier to scale.
2. **Scalability**: Serverless platforms naturally fit with event-driven systems because they automatically scale based on the number of incoming events. For example, AWS Lambda functions can scale automatically to handle large volumes of events from sources like AWS S3, DynamoDB, or SNS (Simple Notification Service).

3. **Asynchronous Processing**: By leveraging asynchronous communication, event-driven systems can improve the responsiveness of the application. Since events are processed in the background, it doesn't block the main user experience. This allows for better user interactions and can reduce the impact of delays in real-time applications.

4. **Improved Fault Tolerance**: In an event-driven system, if one service fails, the others are often unaffected. This is because services are decoupled, and events can be processed asynchronously or even stored for later consumption. This makes the system more resilient to failures and ensures that one point of failure does not bring down the entire system.

5. **Real-Time Processing**: Event-driven architecture supports real-time data processing, which is crucial for use cases like notifications, fraud detection, and logging. With serverless functions, you can instantly trigger reactions to events, enabling real-time updates in your applications.

Challenges of Event-Driven Architecture:

1. **Complexity in Event Management**: Managing and maintaining events, especially as the number of services and event sources increases, can become complex. Ensuring that events are properly routed, stored, and processed without loss requires a robust event handling system.

2. **Eventual Consistency**: Event-driven systems often operate with eventual consistency, meaning that updates across services might not be immediate. For certain use cases, such as financial transactions, this may not be acceptable, and developers will need to consider strategies to manage consistency.

3. **Debugging and Tracing**: Tracking events and debugging event-driven systems can be more challenging than traditional monolithic systems. As events traverse multiple services, maintaining visibility across the entire flow becomes crucial. Distributed tracing and monitoring tools are necessary to provide insights into how events are processed and where failures occur.

Popular Event-Driven Technologies for Serverless:

- **AWS SNS and SQS**: Amazon's messaging services, SNS for pub/sub event broadcasting and SQS for queue-based communication.
- **Google Cloud Pub/Sub**: A scalable messaging system that allows different services to publish and subscribe to events.
- **Azure Event Grid**: A fully managed event routing service that supports integration with Azure Functions.

Event-Driven Architecture is ideal for building highly decoupled, scalable, and resilient serverless applications. It facilitates real-time processing, enhances fault tolerance, and allows services to be more modular and flexible.

5.2 The Bulkhead Pattern: Isolating Failures for Resilience

The **Bulkhead Pattern** is a design pattern borrowed from maritime terminology. In shipbuilding, bulkheads are watertight partitions that divide a ship into sections. The idea is that if one section of the ship is damaged, the rest of the ship remains intact and unaffected. In a microservices architecture, the Bulkhead Pattern is used to isolate failures in individual services to ensure that the failure does not affect other services in the system.

What Is the Bulkhead Pattern? In microservices, services are often distributed across different containers or serverless functions, and they might rely on shared resources such as databases or messaging queues. If one service fails and causes a resource to be overwhelmed, the **Bulkhead Pattern** helps to ensure that other services continue functioning without disruption. It achieves this by isolating critical resources and using them exclusively within individual services or service groups.

In a serverless environment, the Bulkhead Pattern can be applied by isolating different serverless functions or resources to limit the blast radius of a failure. For example, if one serverless function faces a high volume of requests, it can be isolated so that the performance of other functions is not impacted.

Key Benefits of the Bulkhead Pattern in Serverless Systems:

1. **Fault Isolation**: The Bulkhead Pattern ensures that the failure of one component or service does not affect others. In serverless environments, where resources are shared among different functions, isolating functions from each other helps to protect the system's overall stability. For example, if a single function experiences high latency, the isolated resources ensure other functions maintain their performance.
2. **Improved Resilience**: By creating partitions, the Bulkhead Pattern helps to localize the impact of failure. If a service experiences a resource bottleneck or crashes, only the affected partition is impacted. The rest of the system continues to function normally, which improves the overall resilience of the application.
3. **Scalable Resources**: The pattern allows resources to be allocated separately for different components. In serverless systems, each service or function can be allocated specific resources based on its usage pattern. If one service requires more resources, it can be provisioned without affecting other services. This ensures that the system can scale efficiently without service degradation.
4. **Better Control over Resource Consumption**: The Bulkhead Pattern provides better control over resource usage. Since different services or functions are isolated, developers can ensure that resources like memory, CPU, or database connections are allocated appropriately, preventing one service from monopolizing shared resources.

Challenges of the Bulkhead Pattern:

1. **Increased Complexity in Resource Management**: While the Bulkhead Pattern provides benefits in terms of isolation, it can also lead to more complex resource management. For example, ensuring that each microservice has the necessary

resources and does not over-provision them can require more careful planning and monitoring.

2. **Overhead of Service Isolation**: Isolating services may introduce overhead in terms of deployment, management, and monitoring. In serverless environments, each service or function needs to be independently managed, which could increase operational complexity.

3. **Limits on Resource Sharing**: In some cases, it may be necessary for different services to share resources. The Bulkhead Pattern might complicate this, especially when scaling components that require shared resources like databases or queues.

Common Implementations of the Bulkhead Pattern:

- **Serverless Architectures**: Each serverless function can be isolated with its own set of resources to prevent the failure of one from affecting others.
- **Microservices in Containers**: Microservices deployed in containers (e.g., Docker) can be isolated using Kubernetes namespaces to separate resource consumption.

The Bulkhead Pattern is particularly valuable in serverless systems, as it ensures that a failure in one part of the system does not cause cascading failures. By carefully isolating resources, it enhances resilience and scalability in distributed systems.

5.3 The Circuit Breaker Pattern: Preventing System Failures

The **Circuit Breaker Pattern** is a design pattern that helps prevent the failure of one service from cascading and bringing down the entire system. It works by detecting failures early and breaking the chain of service calls to prevent further strain on the system. The concept is similar to an electrical circuit breaker that cuts off the power supply to prevent electrical overload.

What Is the Circuit Breaker Pattern? In a distributed system, one service failure can trigger a chain reaction that leads to the failure of other services, known as a "cascading failure." The Circuit Breaker Pattern helps mitigate this risk by monitoring the health of services and "tripping" the circuit when a service is failing, preventing further calls to it.

When a service repeatedly fails (due to issues like high latency or crashes), the circuit breaker detects this and "opens" the circuit. This prevents additional requests from being sent to the failing service, allowing it to recover without becoming overwhelmed. After a predefined amount of time, the circuit breaker "closes" and allows traffic to flow to the service again, but only after checking if the service has recovered.

Key Benefits of the Circuit Breaker Pattern in Serverless Systems:

1. **Failure Detection and Prevention**: The Circuit Breaker Pattern allows systems to detect failures early and prevent them from spreading throughout the application. In serverless systems, where services are distributed and loosely coupled, this pattern helps to avoid cascading failures, ensuring that other services remain operational even when one is struggling.

2. **Improved System Stability**: By preventing excessive requests from reaching a failing service, the Circuit Breaker Pattern helps maintain system stability. Serverless functions are often designed to scale automatically, but if one function fails repeatedly, it can exhaust system resources. The circuit breaker prevents this by stopping the flood of requests.

3. **Reduced Latency During Failures**: When a service is down, retrying requests without proper handling can increase latency and degrade the performance of the system. The Circuit Breaker Pattern eliminates this by immediately rejecting requests, avoiding the additional time spent trying to reach a failing service.

4. **Graceful Degradation**: Instead of failing entirely, the system can handle failures more gracefully. For example, when the circuit breaker is open, a fallback mechanism can be triggered, such as serving a cached response or providing a

default message. This ensures the system continues functioning in a degraded state rather than becoming entirely unresponsive.

Challenges of the Circuit Breaker Pattern:

1. **Overhead in Management**: Implementing a circuit breaker introduces additional complexity in terms of monitoring and configuration. Developers need to define thresholds for failure detection, such as how many failed requests trigger the circuit breaker and how long the service should be allowed to recover before it is eligible for traffic again.
2. **Configuring the Thresholds**: Setting the correct thresholds for the circuit breaker to trip can be tricky. If the thresholds are too sensitive, the circuit breaker might open prematurely and prevent legitimate traffic from reaching the service. If the thresholds are too lenient, the system might continue trying to reach a failing service, leading to cascading failures.

Common Implementations of the Circuit Breaker Pattern:

- **Netflix Hystrix**: A popular library for implementing circuit breakers in microservices, providing a way to monitor and control service calls.
- **Resilience4j**: A lightweight alternative to Hystrix, focused on fault tolerance for Java-based microservices.
- **AWS Lambda Destinations**: AWS Lambda provides built-in error handling and retry mechanisms that can serve as a form of circuit breaking for serverless applications.

The Circuit Breaker Pattern is crucial for maintaining system reliability and preventing cascading failures, especially in highly distributed environments like serverless microservices.

5.4 The Retry Pattern: Improving Reliability in Serverless Functions

The **Retry Pattern** is a design pattern used to automatically attempt an operation again if it fails due to a transient error. This pattern is particularly important in serverless systems, where operations may occasionally fail due to temporary network issues, service unavailability, or timeouts.

What Is the Retry Pattern? The Retry Pattern involves automatically retrying a failed operation after a short delay. The operation is retried a predefined number of times, with the hope that the error will be resolved by the time the next attempt is made. In serverless systems, where functions are stateless and may depend on external services (such as databases or APIs), transient failures are common, and retrying is often an effective way to increase reliability.

The retry mechanism typically involves adding exponential backoff between attempts, gradually increasing the delay between each retry to avoid overwhelming the system or service being called.

Key Benefits of the Retry Pattern in Serverless Systems:

1. **Increased Reliability**: By automatically retrying failed operations, the Retry Pattern increases the reliability of serverless functions, especially in cases where failures are caused by temporary issues, such as network latency or external service unavailability.

2. **Reduced Impact of Temporary Failures**: Many external services and systems experience occasional transient failures. The Retry Pattern ensures that temporary issues don't lead to a permanent failure in the system, improving the robustness of the application.

3. **Cost-Effective**: In serverless environments, where you pay only for the execution time of functions, retrying operations is a cost-effective way to handle transient errors. Serverless functions can be configured with retry logic to

prevent wasted resources on failed requests, ensuring that only successful requests result in additional compute charges.

4. **Improved User Experience**: When failures occur, retrying them automatically helps maintain a smooth user experience. For example, if a user's request is temporarily delayed due to a service outage, retries ensure that the request can be fulfilled without user intervention, reducing the likelihood of error messages or failed transactions.

Challenges of the Retry Pattern:

1. **Handling Idempotency**: The main challenge of the Retry Pattern is ensuring that the operation being retried is **idempotent**. This means that if the operation is retried multiple times, it should not cause unintended side effects, such as duplicated transactions or data corruption. For example, retrying a payment operation could result in double charges if the system does not handle retries correctly.

2. **Exponential Backoff**: While exponential backoff helps reduce the strain on a service during retries, determining the optimal delay and maximum number of retries can be difficult. Setting the retry parameters too aggressively can overwhelm the service, while setting them too conservatively might lead to unnecessary delays.

3. **Monitoring and Alerting**: It's essential to monitor and alert on retry operations to avoid situations where retries are unsuccessful and create excessive load on the system. Without proper monitoring, retrying errors might go unnoticed, resulting in system overload or resource exhaustion.

Common Implementations of the Retry Pattern:

- **AWS SDK Retry Logic**: AWS SDK includes built-in retry logic for handling transient errors when interacting with AWS services.
- **Azure Functions**: Azure provides built-in retry policies for functions that interact with external services or APIs.

70

- **Resilience4j**: A Java library that provides retry functionality, including exponential backoff, for microservices.

The Retry Pattern is a simple yet effective way to improve reliability in serverless systems, particularly in environments where external dependencies might occasionally fail. It enhances the overall resilience of applications by ensuring that temporary issues don't lead to permanent failures.

5.5 The Cache-Aside Pattern: Speeding Up Serverless Operations

In serverless architectures, performance is critical, especially when responding to user requests in real-time. One common challenge is that fetching data from external systems, like databases or APIs, can introduce latency. The **Cache-Aside Pattern** addresses this challenge by leveraging an external caching layer to store frequently accessed data, reducing the need for expensive or time-consuming queries on every request.

What Is the Cache-Aside Pattern? The **Cache-Aside Pattern** is a caching strategy where the application (or in the case of serverless, the function) is responsible for loading data into the cache when it is needed, as well as checking the cache before querying the data store. This pattern works by storing data in the cache on-demand and ensuring that subsequent requests can quickly retrieve data from the cache, avoiding the overhead of repeated data fetches from a backend system like a database.

The cache acts as an intermediary between the client (or the serverless function) and the data source, providing fast access to frequently requested data. The application (or function) checks the cache first, and if the data is not found, it retrieves the data from the original source, updates the cache, and returns the result to the user.

Key Benefits of the Cache-Aside Pattern in Serverless Systems:

1. **Improved Performance**:
   The Cache-Aside Pattern significantly improves response times by serving data

71

from memory rather than fetching it from slower external sources like databases or APIs. For serverless functions, this means faster execution, reduced latency, and a better user experience.

2. **Reduced Load on Backend Systems**:

   By caching frequently accessed data, the Cache-Aside Pattern reduces the number of requests that need to be processed by backend systems. This can lower the load on databases, APIs, or external services, reducing operational costs and improving overall system efficiency.

3. **Scalability**:

   Serverless environments automatically scale based on demand, and caching can help reduce the strain on these backend systems by offloading data retrieval to a fast, in-memory cache. This is particularly valuable during traffic spikes, as caching helps maintain system performance without adding additional stress to backend systems.

4. **Flexibility**:

   The Cache-Aside Pattern offers flexibility by allowing developers to choose what data is cached. Data that is frequently accessed or expensive to compute (e.g., popular product details, user profiles, etc.) can be cached, while less frequently requested data can be excluded from the cache.

Challenges of the Cache-Aside Pattern:

1. **Cache Invalidation**:

   One of the primary challenges with the Cache-Aside Pattern is ensuring that the cache remains up-to-date. When data in the original source changes, the cache must be invalidated or updated to reflect those changes. Without proper cache invalidation mechanisms, the application might serve stale data, leading to inconsistent or incorrect responses.

2. **Memory Management**:

   Managing the cache's memory and ensuring it doesn't grow too large or consume excessive resources can be tricky. When implementing the

Cache-Aside Pattern, it's important to define eviction policies (e.g., Least Recently Used or LRU) to remove old or infrequently accessed data and avoid cache bloat.

3. **Cache Misses**:

Cache misses occur when the requested data is not found in the cache and must be fetched from the original data source. Handling cache misses efficiently and ensuring that data retrieval from the backend is optimized is critical to prevent performance degradation.

Common Implementations of the Cache-Aside Pattern:

- **AWS ElastiCache**: A fully managed in-memory data store that works with Redis or Memcached, often used for caching frequently accessed data in serverless applications.
- **Google Cloud Memorystore**: A fully managed Redis and Memcached service that provides fast caching for data-heavy serverless applications.
- **Azure Cache for Redis**: A scalable, in-memory data store that can be integrated with Azure Functions to improve the performance of serverless applications by caching frequently accessed data.

The Cache-Aside Pattern is a powerful way to speed up serverless operations by caching frequently requested data, improving performance and reducing load on backend systems.

5.6 The Throttling Pattern: Managing Load in Serverless Architectures

Serverless architectures, by their nature, scale automatically in response to demand. However, when an application receives an unexpectedly high volume of requests, it can quickly overwhelm downstream services or third-party APIs. The **Throttling Pattern** is a key strategy for managing this load and ensuring that your system remains performant and reliable under heavy traffic.

What Is Throttling? Throttling refers to controlling the rate at which requests are processed. The Throttling Pattern involves limiting the number of requests to a service, ensuring that resources are not overwhelmed. In a serverless environment, this can be especially useful to avoid excessive function invocations, API calls, or database requests, which could increase costs or degrade performance.

Throttling is typically implemented by setting rate limits or quotas for requests. When the limit is exceeded, the system can either reject the request, queue it for later processing, or apply a delay before allowing additional requests to be processed.

Key Benefits of the Throttling Pattern in Serverless Systems:

1. **Prevention of Service Overload**:
   Throttling helps prevent backend services or serverless functions from being overwhelmed during periods of high traffic. By limiting the rate of requests, you ensure that the system can handle spikes in load without crashing or slowing down.

2. **Cost Control**:
   Serverless functions typically incur costs based on the number of executions and the execution time. By implementing throttling, you can control the rate at which functions are invoked, ensuring that you don't exceed budgetary limits during high-demand periods.

3. **Improved User Experience**:
   Throttling can help manage user expectations by providing consistent and predictable response times. For instance, when traffic spikes occur, throttling ensures that the system can still respond to user requests in a controlled manner, avoiding system crashes or unresponsiveness.

4. **Fair Resource Distribution**:
   Throttling ensures that no single user or client consumes excessive resources. This is particularly important when there are many users or clients interacting

with the system simultaneously. By limiting the rate of access, you ensure fair usage and maintain the integrity of your service.

Challenges of the Throttling Pattern:

1. **Handling Rate Limits Gracefully**:
   When the rate limit is exceeded, it's essential to handle the response gracefully. If requests are rejected without explanation, users might experience frustration or confusion. Implementing a polite error message or redirecting users to a waiting queue is important to improve user experience.

2. **Exponential Backoff**:
   In some cases, retrying a request after a brief delay may lead to further congestion, creating a feedback loop of retries that causes the system to become even more overwhelmed. Implementing **exponential backoff** or a similar strategy for retries helps mitigate this issue by gradually increasing the delay between retry attempts.

3. **Defining Appropriate Limits**:
   Setting the correct throttling thresholds can be challenging. If the limit is set too low, it may result in unnecessary rejections, frustrating users. If it's too high, the system may still become overloaded. Fine-tuning the throttling parameters requires continuous monitoring and adjustment based on traffic patterns.

Common Implementations of the Throttling Pattern:

- **API Gateway Throttling**: API gateways like AWS API Gateway and Google Cloud API Gateway offer built-in rate limiting and throttling features to limit the number of requests that can be made to an API endpoint.
- **AWS Lambda Concurrency Limits**: AWS Lambda allows developers to set concurrency limits on functions, ensuring that a function doesn't process more requests than it can handle at once.

By implementing the **Throttling Pattern**, serverless applications can efficiently manage traffic, prevent system overload, control costs, and improve user satisfaction during high-demand periods.

5.7 The Back-Pressure Pattern: Controlling System Flow

The **Back-Pressure Pattern** is an advanced technique used to manage the flow of data or requests in a system, particularly when the system is under stress or facing resource constraints. When a system is experiencing high load or processing too many requests, back-pressure is used to slow down the flow of data or requests to prevent the system from becoming overwhelmed.

What Is Back-Pressure? Back-pressure is a mechanism for controlling the rate at which data or requests flow through a system. When a system reaches its capacity, back-pressure signals upstream components to reduce or pause the flow of requests until the system can catch up. This prevents the system from becoming overloaded and ensures that resources are used efficiently.

In serverless systems, where functions scale automatically based on demand, back-pressure is crucial for managing how data flows between services. For example, if one serverless function is overwhelmed with requests, back-pressure can ensure that incoming events are queued or delayed until the system can process them.

Key Benefits of the Back-Pressure Pattern in Serverless Systems:

1. **System Stability**:
   The Back-Pressure Pattern ensures that the system remains stable under heavy load by controlling the rate at which requests are processed. This helps prevent overloading and ensures that the system can continue operating without crashing or degrading performance.

2. **Prevention of Resource Exhaustion**:
   In serverless environments, excessive function invocations can lead to resource

exhaustion, resulting in higher costs or degraded performance. Back-pressure helps manage the rate of function invocations, preventing unnecessary function executions that could deplete resources.

3. **Optimized Resource Utilization**:

Back-pressure ensures that serverless functions or microservices do not process more data than they can handle at a given time. This improves the overall efficiency of the system by preventing overuse of compute resources, network bandwidth, or other critical resources.

4. **Graceful Degradation**:

Instead of rejecting requests or allowing the system to fail abruptly, back-pressure provides a way to slow down the flow of data and allow the system to gracefully handle high load. This helps maintain user satisfaction even during periods of high demand.

Challenges of the Back-Pressure Pattern:

1. **Complexity in Implementation**:

Implementing back-pressure requires careful design, especially when dealing with distributed systems. Coordinating the flow of data and ensuring that all components of the system respond to back-pressure signals properly can be complex.

2. **Latency**:

Back-pressure may introduce latency as it reduces the rate of requests or processes. While this prevents system overload, it can lead to delays in processing, which might negatively affect user experience, especially in real-time applications.

3. **Effective Communication**:

Proper communication between components is required to implement back-pressure effectively. If one component signals back-pressure but the other components fail to respond appropriately, it could lead to cascading failures or inefficiencies.

Common Implementations of the Back-Pressure Pattern:

- **Messaging Queues**: Systems like AWS SQS, Kafka, or Google Pub/Sub can be used to implement back-pressure by queuing messages when the system is under load, ensuring that they are processed later when the system has capacity.
- **Flow Control in HTTP APIs**: In HTTP-based APIs, back-pressure can be implemented by using rate-limiting headers or pausing requests when the server is overwhelmed.
- **Serverless Event Queues**: Using event-driven architectures and queues, such as AWS Lambda with SQS or Google Cloud Functions with Pub/Sub, allows for natural implementation of back-pressure by temporarily storing events until they can be processed.

By using the **Back-Pressure Pattern**, serverless architectures can ensure that data and requests are processed efficiently, preventing resource exhaustion, ensuring system stability, and maintaining performance even during periods of high load.

Chapter 6: Hands-On Implementation of Serverless Design Patterns

6.1 Setting Up Your Development Environment for Serverless Applications

Before diving into hands-on implementation, it's essential to set up a development environment tailored for serverless applications. The right tools and configurations will help streamline the development process, enhance productivity, and ensure a smooth deployment.

1. Install the Serverless Framework

The **Serverless Framework** is a popular open-source tool that simplifies the deployment of serverless applications. It supports AWS, Google Cloud, Azure, and other cloud providers. To install the Serverless Framework, follow these steps:

- Install Node.js (which comes with npm) from Node.js website.

Install the Serverless Framework globally by running the following command in your terminal:

Copy

```
npm install -g serverless
```

- Verify the installation by checking the version:

    css

    Copy

    ```
    serverless --version
    ```

2. Set Up Your Cloud Provider Credentials

For deploying serverless applications to AWS, you need to configure your AWS credentials. The most common way is by using the **AWS CLI** (Command Line Interface).

- Install AWS CLI from AWS CLI Installation Guide.

Configure the AWS CLI by running:

Copy

```
aws configure
```

- This will prompt you to enter your AWS Access Key, Secret Key, Region, and Output format. If you don't have these credentials, you can create them in the **IAM Console** under your AWS account.

3. Set Up an Integrated Development Environment (IDE)

While you can use any text editor or IDE, it's beneficial to use one that supports serverless development with features such as syntax highlighting, code completion, and debugging. Popular choices for serverless applications include:

- **Visual Studio Code**: A lightweight, powerful IDE with a wide range of extensions, including support for AWS and serverless development.
- **JetBrains IntelliJ IDEA**: A full-featured IDE that offers a plugin for AWS Lambda and serverless development.

You may also install the necessary extensions for AWS Lambda, CloudFormation, or serverless frameworks to help speed up development.

4. Local Development Tools for Serverless

For a seamless development and testing experience, it's crucial to use tools that emulate cloud environments locally. These tools allow you to run and test serverless functions on your machine before deploying them to the cloud.

Serverless Offline Plugin: The Serverless Offline plugin simulates AWS API Gateway and AWS Lambda locally, allowing you to run and test serverless functions in your local environment.

Install the plugin:

css

Copy

```
npm install serverless-offline --save-dev
```

- **LocalStack**: LocalStack is a fully functional local AWS cloud stack that allows you to test AWS services locally. It's particularly helpful for local testing of DynamoDB, S3, Lambda, and other AWS services.

Install LocalStack via Docker:

bash

Copy

```
docker pull localstack/localstack
```

With these tools in place, you are ready to develop, test, and deploy serverless applications effectively.

6.2 Deploying Microservices with AWS Lambda

AWS Lambda is at the core of serverless computing. Lambda lets you run code without provisioning or managing servers. The code you upload to Lambda is executed in response to events from other AWS services or external sources, making it perfect for microservices architecture.

1. Create a New Serverless Project

Let's start by creating a new serverless project using the Serverless Framework.

Run the following command to create a new project:

css

Copy

```
serverless create --template aws-nodejs --path my-serverless-project
cd my-serverless-project
```

This creates a simple project structure with the necessary configuration file (serverless.yml) and a sample Lambda function.

2. Define the Lambda Function

Edit the serverless.yml file to define the Lambda function. Below is an example of how you can define a simple Lambda function that responds to HTTP requests via AWS API Gateway:

yaml

Copy

```yaml
service: my-serverless-app

provider:
  name: aws
  runtime: nodejs14.x

functions:
  hello:
    handler: handler.hello
    events:
      - http:
          path: hello
          method: get
```

In the handler.js file, define the Lambda function:

82

javascript

Copy

```
module.exports.hello = async (event) => {
  return {
    statusCode: 200,
    body: JSON.stringify(
      {
        message: 'Hello, Serverless!',
        input: event,
      },
      null,
      2
    ),
  };
};
```

3. Deploy the Lambda Function

Once the function is defined, deploy the application to AWS:

Copy

```
serverless deploy
```

The Serverless Framework will package your function, deploy it to AWS Lambda, and set up the necessary infrastructure (like API Gateway). After deployment, you'll get an endpoint URL where your Lambda function is accessible.

4. Test the Lambda Function

After deployment, you can test the Lambda function by visiting the provided URL in your browser or using a tool like Postman to send a GET request to the endpoint.

83

6.3 Implementing the API Gateway Pattern with AWS API Gateway

API Gateway serves as a central point for managing all client interactions with your serverless functions. It routes HTTP requests to AWS Lambda or other backend services.

1. Define API Gateway in Serverless Configuration

In the serverless.yml file, the API Gateway integration has already been defined as part of the Lambda function (events: http). Let's expand this example to handle multiple routes and methods.

Here's an updated version of serverless.yml:

yaml

Copy

```
service: my-serverless-app

provider:
  name: aws
  runtime: nodejs14.x

functions:
  hello:
    handler: handler.hello
    events:
      - http:
          path: hello
          method: get
          cors: true
  greet:
    handler: handler.greet
```

```
events:
  - http:
      path: greet
      method: post
      cors: true
```

Now, **update** handler.js to include the greet **function:**

javascript
Copy
```
module.exports.hello = async (event) => {
  return {
    statusCode: 200,
    body: JSON.stringify(
      {
        message: 'Hello from the API Gateway!',
        input: event,
      },
      null,
      2
    ),
  };
};

module.exports.greet = async (event) => {
  const { name } = JSON.parse(event.body);
  return {
    statusCode: 200,
    body: JSON.stringify({
      message: `Hello, S{name}!`,
```

```
  }),
  };
};
```

2. Deploy and Test the API Gateway

After updating the configuration, deploy the new changes:

Copy

serverless deploy

The Serverless Framework will update the API Gateway routes. You can now test both the GET /hello and POST /greet endpoints by sending requests using a browser or tools like Postman.

6.4 Event Sourcing: Implementing with AWS DynamoDB

Event sourcing is a pattern in which every state change in your system is stored as an event, making it possible to reconstruct the current state by replaying the events.

1. Set Up DynamoDB

First, you need to define DynamoDB as the event store for your application. In the serverless.yml file, define the DynamoDB table:

yaml

Copy

```
service: event-sourcing-app

provider:
  name: aws
  runtime: nodejs14.x
```

86

```yaml
resources:
  Resources:
    EventsTable:
      Type: AWS::DynamoDB::Table
      Properties:
        TableName: Events
        AttributeDefinitions:
          - AttributeName: eventId
            AttributeType: S
        KeySchema:
          - AttributeName: eventId
            KeyType: HASH
        ProvisionedThroughput:
          ReadCapacityUnits: 5
          WriteCapacityUnits: 5

functions:
  createEvent:
    handler: handler.createEvent
    events:
      - http:
          path: events
          method: post
```

2. Implement the Event Sourcing Logic

In the handler.js file, implement the logic to store events in DynamoDB. Each event will have a unique eventId and will store the event details in a table:

javascript

Copy

```javascript
const AWS = require('aws-sdk');
const dynamoDB = new AWS.DynamoDB.DocumentClient();

module.exports.createEvent = async (event) => {
  const { eventName, payload } = JSON.parse(event.body);

  const eventId = new Date().getTime().toString(); // Use timestamp for unique event ID

  const params = {
    TableName: 'Events',
    Item: {
      eventId,
      eventName,
      payload,
      timestamp: new Date().toISOString(),
    },
  };

  try {
    await dynamoDB.put(params).promise();
    return {
      statusCode: 200,
      body: JSON.stringify({
        message: 'Event created successfully',
        eventId,
      }),
    };
  } catch (error) {
    return {
      statusCode: 500,
```

```
  body: JSON.stringify({
    message: 'Failed to create event',
    error: error.message,
  }),
  };
 }
};
```

3. Deploy and Test Event Sourcing

Deploy the function and DynamoDB table:

Copy

```
serverless deploy
```

After deployment, use Postman or curl to send a POST request to the /events endpoint, passing the event data in the request body. The event will be stored in DynamoDB, and you can later retrieve and replay it to reconstruct the state of your system.

4. Retrieve Events

You can implement another Lambda function to retrieve the stored events and replay them:

javascript
Copy

```
module.exports.getEvents = async () => {
  const params = {
    TableName: 'Events',
  };

  try {
```

```javascript
    const data = await dynamoDB.scan(params).promise();
    return {
      statusCode: 200,
      body: JSON.stringify({
        events: data.Items,
      }),
    };
  } catch (error) {
    return {
      statusCode: 500,
      body: JSON.stringify({
        message: 'Failed to retrieve events',
        error: error.message,
      }),
    };
  }
};
```

By implementing **Event Sourcing** with DynamoDB in this way, you can maintain a complete history of state changes, ensuring that your application can recover and reconstruct its state from any point in time.

With these hands-on examples, you now have a working understanding of how to set up serverless applications and implement key design patterns like the **API Gateway Pattern**, **Event Sourcing**, and more. We covered how to use the **Serverless Framework**, **AWS Lambda**, **API Gateway**, and **DynamoDB** to deploy microservices and implement core patterns that are crucial for building scalable, resilient serverless applications.

6.5 Building CQRS with AWS Lambda and DynamoDB

The **CQRS (Command Query Responsibility Segregation)** pattern separates the read and write operations of an application, optimizing each side for its specific workload. In serverless environments, combining AWS Lambda with DynamoDB allows you to easily implement CQRS while leveraging the scalability and efficiency of serverless computing.

1. Set Up DynamoDB for Command and Query Models

Start by defining two different tables in DynamoDB: one for write operations (commands) and another for read operations (queries). This separation allows you to optimize both data models independently.

In the serverless.yml file, define the resources for two DynamoDB tables:

yaml

Copy

```yaml
resources:
  Resources:
    WriteTable:
      Type: AWS::DynamoDB::Table
      Properties:
        TableName: WriteTable
        AttributeDefinitions:
          - AttributeName: eventId
            AttributeType: S
        KeySchema:
          - AttributeName: eventId
            KeyType: HASH
        ProvisionedThroughput:
          ReadCapacityUnits: 5
```

```
            WriteCapacityUnits: 5

      ReadTable:
        Type: AWS::DynamoDB::Table
        Properties:
          TableName: ReadTable
          AttributeDefinitions:
            - AttributeName: userId
              AttributeType: S
          KeySchema:
            - AttributeName: userId
              KeyType: HASH
          ProvisionedThroughput:
            ReadCapacityUnits: 5
            WriteCapacityUnits: 5
```

2. Define Command and Query Lambda Functions

In the handler.js file, define two functions: one for handling write commands and the other for handling read queries.

For the **write function**, which processes commands:

javascript

Copy

```javascript
const AWS = require('aws-sdk');
const dynamoDB = new AWS.DynamoDB.DocumentClient();

module.exports.createUser = async (event) => {
  const { userId, name, email } = JSON.parse(event.body);
```

```javascript
const params = {
  TableName: 'WriteTable',
  Item: {
    eventId: new Date().toISOString(),
    userId,
    name,
    email,
  },
};

try {
  await dynamoDB.put(params).promise();
  return {
    statusCode: 200,
    body: JSON.stringify({ message: 'User created successfully!' }),
  };
} catch (error) {
  return {
    statusCode: 500,
    body: JSON.stringify({ message: 'Failed to create user', error }),
  };
}
};
```

For the **query function**, which reads data from the read-optimized table:

javascript

Copy

```javascript
module.exports.getUser = async (event) => {
  const userId = event.pathParameters.userId;
```

```
const params = {
  TableName: 'ReadTable',
  Key: {
    userId,
  },
};

try {
  const data = await dynamoDB.get(params).promise();
  if (!data.Item) {
    return { statusCode: 404, body: JSON.stringify({ message: 'User not found' }) };
  }

  return {
    statusCode: 200,
    body: JSON.stringify(data.Item),
  };
} catch (error) {
  return {
    statusCode: 500,
    body: JSON.stringify({ message: 'Failed to retrieve user', error }),
  };
}
};
```

3. Implementing Eventual Consistency

In a CQRS implementation, the read model is eventually consistent. The createUser function writes data to the **WriteTable**, and then a separate process or event triggers the update of the **ReadTable**. You can use AWS Lambda with DynamoDB Streams to replicate data from the write table to the read table asynchronously, ensuring eventual consistency.

4. Deploy and Test

Deploy the application using the Serverless Framework:

Copy
```
serverless deploy
```

Once deployed, you can test the POST /user endpoint for the command and the GET /user/{userId} endpoint for the query. The write operation will populate the **WriteTable**, and the read operation will retrieve data from the **ReadTable**.

6.6 Building a Resilient System with the Circuit Breaker Pattern

The **Circuit Breaker Pattern** is crucial for maintaining system stability in the face of failure. In serverless systems, where services are highly distributed, the Circuit Breaker Pattern helps prevent cascading failures by stopping requests to services that are already failing.

1. Use AWS Lambda Destinations for Error Handling

AWS Lambda provides built-in support for destinations, which allows you to specify a target for handling the success or failure of Lambda executions. By combining this with the Circuit Breaker Pattern, you can redirect failed requests to a fallback mechanism or notify an administrator when failures occur.

In your serverless.yml, configure a **dead-letter queue** or a **failure destination** for Lambda functions:

yaml
Copy

```
functions:
  processPayment:
    handler: handler.processPayment
    maximumRetryAttempts: 2
    destination:
      onFailure: arn:aws:sqs:REGION:ACCOUNT_ID:PaymentFailureQueue
```

2. Implement a Custom Circuit Breaker Logic

While AWS doesn't have a built-in Circuit Breaker service, you can implement the logic within your Lambda functions. For instance, you could monitor failure rates and manually trip the circuit after a certain number of failures.

Here's an example of how you might implement a simple circuit breaker in handler.js:

javascript

Copy

```
let failureCount = 0;
const failureThreshold = 3; // The circuit will break after 3 consecutive failures

module.exports.processPayment = async (event) => {
  if (failureCount >= failureThreshold) {
    return {
      statusCode: 503,
      body: JSON.stringify({ message: 'Circuit breaker is open. Please try again later.' }),
    };
  }

  try {
    // Payment processing logic
    const paymentSuccess = await processPaymentLogic(event);
```

```
    return {
      statusCode: 200,
      body: JSON.stringify({ message: 'Payment processed successfully!' }),
    };
  } catch (error) {
    failureCount++;
    return {
      statusCode: 500,
      body: JSON.stringify({ message: 'Payment processing failed', error }),
    };
  }
};
```

3. Monitoring and Resetting the Circuit

After a failure threshold is reached, the circuit can be opened, and requests will be rejected or routed to fallback logic. However, the circuit breaker should automatically reset after a set period, allowing traffic to flow again once the service has recovered.

4. Testing

Deploy the function using the Serverless Framework and simulate failures to test the circuit breaker logic. Use AWS CloudWatch Logs to monitor the failure count and track when the circuit is tripped and reset.

6.7 Integrating the Bulkhead Pattern in Serverless Functions

The **Bulkhead Pattern** in serverless applications ensures that failures are isolated to a single component or service, preventing cascading failures. This is particularly important in systems with multiple serverless functions that may share resources.

97

1. Isolate Function Resources

In AWS Lambda, the Bulkhead Pattern can be implemented by setting function concurrency limits. This ensures that one function's load does not impact the performance of others.

In your serverless.yml file, set the concurrency configuration for a Lambda function:

yaml

Copy

```
functions:
  processOrder:
    handler: handler.processOrder
    reservedConcurrency: 5  # Only allow 5 concurrent executions
```

This ensures that the processOrder function has a maximum of 5 concurrent executions, isolating it from other functions that might consume resources.

2. Manage Resource Sharing

For shared resources, such as databases or external APIs, you can implement a **separate connection pool** for each service. By doing so, you prevent any one service from overwhelming shared resources, helping maintain stability.

For example, in a serverless architecture where multiple functions interact with a DynamoDB table, use unique partition keys or different access patterns to ensure that the load is distributed evenly.

3. Test the Isolation

Once you've set up the Bulkhead Pattern, test the system by simulating a heavy load on one service and monitoring how other services behave. Ensure that functions with reserved concurrency limits are properly isolated and that the overall system maintains stability.

6.8 Building Reliable and Scalable APIs with Serverless Technologies

Building reliable and scalable APIs is a key use case for serverless technologies. AWS Lambda, API Gateway, and other serverless components allow you to quickly scale API endpoints without worrying about infrastructure management.

1. Set Up API Gateway for Multiple Endpoints

To create a scalable and reliable API, use **AWS API Gateway** to define multiple endpoints that trigger different Lambda functions. In your serverless.yml, define the API Gateway configuration as follows:

yaml

Copy

```yaml
functions:
  createUser:
    handler: handler.createUser
    events:
      - http:
          path: users
          method: post
  getUser:
    handler: handler.getUser
    events:
      - http:
          path: users/{userId}
          method: get
```

This configuration sets up two API endpoints: one to create a user (POST /users) and another to retrieve a user (GET /users/{userId}).

2. Add API Gateway Features

API Gateway offers many features to enhance your API, including **rate limiting**, **authentication**, **CORS configuration**, and more. You can configure these features directly in your serverless.yml file.

For example, to enable rate limiting and CORS for an endpoint:

yaml

Copy

```
functions:
  createUser:
    handler: handler.createUser
    events:
      - http:
          path: users
          method: post
          cors: true
          throttling:
            burstLimit: 200
            rateLimit: 100
```

This ensures that the POST /users endpoint can handle a burst of 200 requests and a steady rate of 100 requests per second.

3. Ensure API Reliability

In addition to scaling automatically, serverless APIs can be made more reliable by using patterns like **Circuit Breaker** and **Throttling**. For example, API Gateway can throttle excessive traffic, ensuring that downstream services aren't overwhelmed.

Additionally, you can implement a **Retry Pattern** using Lambda destinations and set up Lambda retry policies to handle transient failures.

100

4. Monitoring and Logging

Serverless APIs should be monitored to ensure reliability. AWS CloudWatch provides monitoring for Lambda functions and API Gateway, so you can track the number of requests, response times, errors, and more.

Set up CloudWatch logs and create custom metrics to monitor the health of your serverless API. Use these insights to continuously improve your API's performance and reliability.

By combining serverless technologies with best practices such as **scalability**, **reliability**, and **monitoring**, you can build a robust, scalable API that can handle heavy loads without requiring

Chapter 7: Case Studies and Real-World Applications

7.1 Case Study 1: Serverless Microservices for E-commerce

E-commerce platforms have unique challenges due to fluctuating traffic loads, the need for high availability, and the requirement for fast, responsive systems. Implementing a serverless architecture for an e-commerce system can greatly enhance scalability and reliability while reducing operational complexity and cost.

Scenario: Imagine an e-commerce platform that processes thousands of transactions daily, managing inventory, orders, customer data, payments, and shipping. A traditional monolithic architecture might struggle to scale with traffic spikes during peak shopping periods (e.g., Black Friday). However, by moving to serverless microservices, we can decompose the platform into independent services that scale automatically based on demand.

Serverless Microservices Components:

1. **AWS Lambda**: AWS Lambda functions handle various tasks in the e-commerce platform:
   - **Product Management**: Updating product details and inventory in the database.
   - **Order Processing**: Triggering payment and shipment actions once an order is confirmed.
   - **Customer Management**: Storing user profiles, preferences, and transaction history.
2. **API Gateway**: API Gateway serves as the entry point for all client interactions. It routes requests to the appropriate Lambda functions and handles authentication and rate-limiting, ensuring that backend services are not overwhelmed during traffic surges.

3. **DynamoDB for Data Storage**: DynamoDB is used for storing product information, customer data, and order details in a distributed, highly available database. The **Database per Service** pattern is employed to ensure each microservice has its own database schema, reducing data coupling and improving scalability.

4. **S3 for Media Storage**: Product images and videos are stored in AWS S3. Serverless functions trigger S3 events to update product listings whenever new media is uploaded.

5. **SNS and SQS for Messaging**:
   - **SNS** (Simple Notification Service) is used to send real-time notifications to customers about order updates, promotions, or abandoned carts.
   - **SQS** (Simple Queue Service) is used for decoupling order processing tasks. When a new order is placed, a message is placed in the queue to be processed by Lambda functions.

Benefits:

1. **Scalability**: Each Lambda function automatically scales based on traffic, ensuring that the e-commerce platform can handle high demand during peak shopping times.

2. **Cost-Efficiency**: The pay-per-use model of AWS Lambda means that the platform only incurs charges based on actual usage, reducing costs significantly compared to maintaining dedicated infrastructure.

3. **High Availability**: Serverless services are inherently fault-tolerant. If one Lambda function fails, the failure won't affect others, and the platform can continue to function.

4. **Faster Time to Market**: Developers can quickly build and deploy individual services, speeding up the release of new features and updates.

Challenges:

- **Eventual Consistency**: With a distributed system, ensuring data consistency across multiple services can be challenging. Techniques like **Event Sourcing** and **CQRS** are implemented to ensure eventual consistency between microservices.
- **Cold Starts**: AWS Lambda functions may experience slight delays during the cold start process. These delays can be minimized with optimization strategies such as keeping critical functions warm.

7.2 Case Study 2: Financial Transactions in Serverless Systems

Financial systems require high security, low latency, and reliability due to the sensitive nature of transactions and the need for real-time processing. Serverless computing, while offering scalability and flexibility, needs to be implemented carefully to meet these requirements.

Scenario: A global financial institution processes millions of transactions daily, ranging from payments to account transfers. The platform needs to scale to handle sudden spikes in transaction volume during periods of high demand while maintaining stringent security and compliance standards.

Serverless Components in the Financial System:

1. **AWS Lambda**: Lambda functions process various types of financial transactions:
   - **Payment Processing**: Validating payment details, initiating bank transfers, and handling fraud detection.
   - **Account Management**: Updating account balances and transaction history.
   - **Compliance Checks**: Ensuring that transactions meet regulatory requirements (e.g., Anti-Money Laundering checks).

2. **API Gateway**: API Gateway routes external client requests (e.g., from mobile apps or web interfaces) to appropriate Lambda functions, ensuring secure access to the financial system. AWS Cognito is integrated for authentication and authorization.

3. **DynamoDB and RDS**:
    - **DynamoDB** is used for storing transaction logs and non-relational data such as user profiles and session data.
    - **RDS (Relational Database Service)** is used for managing structured transactional data like customer accounts and balances.

4. **SQS and SNS for Event Handling**:
    - **SQS** is used to queue large volumes of incoming transaction requests for asynchronous processing, ensuring that each transaction is handled in the correct order and with adequate system resources.
    - **SNS** sends notifications for successful payments or failed transactions to both customers and internal staff.

5. **AWS KMS (Key Management Service)**: AWS KMS ensures that sensitive data, such as payment details and customer account numbers, is securely encrypted at rest and in transit.

Benefits:

1. **Scalability**: The financial platform automatically scales to handle high transaction volumes during peak times (e.g., end-of-month, holidays).

2. **Cost Reduction**: The pay-as-you-go model of AWS Lambda allows the financial institution to reduce infrastructure costs, only paying for the transactions processed.

3. **Security**: Integration with AWS KMS and Lambda's native support for encryption ensures that sensitive data is always protected. Additionally, Lambda functions can be configured with fine-grained IAM roles for access control.

4. **Reliability**: Serverless functions are highly available and resilient. Failures in one part of the system (e.g., payment processing) don't cause failures in others.

Challenges:

- **Latency**: Financial transactions require low-latency processing to ensure real-time processing. Optimizing serverless functions and using appropriate event-driven architectures minimizes latency.
- **Regulatory Compliance**: Financial systems must meet strict regulatory standards (e.g., GDPR, PCI DSS). Ensuring compliance while maintaining a serverless architecture requires careful design, especially regarding data storage and encryption.

7.3 Case Study 3: Event-Driven IoT Applications

IoT (Internet of Things) applications often involve large-scale distributed devices that send continuous streams of data to be processed and acted upon in real-time. Serverless architectures, particularly event-driven ones, are well-suited to this type of workload, allowing for seamless scalability and cost-effective operation.

Scenario: An industrial IoT company is building a platform to monitor and control thousands of devices (e.g., sensors, machines, and environmental monitors) in a factory. The platform needs to handle incoming data from these devices, process it in real-time, and trigger actions such as sending alerts or adjusting machine settings based on sensor readings.

Serverless IoT Components:

1. **AWS Lambda**:
   - **Data Processing**: Lambda functions process data received from IoT devices. For example, a function may analyze sensor data for temperature or pressure and trigger an alert if values go beyond certain thresholds.
   - **Event Triggering**: Lambda functions trigger actions based on device status or changes in environmental conditions, such as sending notifications to maintenance teams or adjusting device configurations.

2. **AWS IoT Core**: AWS IoT Core allows secure, bidirectional communication between IoT devices and the cloud. Devices send data to AWS IoT Core, which can trigger Lambda functions to process the data.

3. **Amazon Kinesis**: For real-time data streaming, Amazon Kinesis streams data from IoT devices to Lambda functions for processing. Kinesis allows for handling high-throughput streams of data from multiple devices in parallel.

4. **DynamoDB**: DynamoDB is used to store sensor readings, device status, and historical data. Each IoT device can have its own data table, allowing easy access and querying of device-specific data.

5. **SNS for Notifications**: When certain conditions are met (e.g., a sensor detects an anomaly), AWS SNS sends real-time notifications to users or devices to take action (e.g., maintenance crew receives an alert on mobile).

6. **S3 for Data Storage**: Large amounts of IoT data are stored in S3 buckets, providing a durable, cost-effective storage solution for logs, historical sensor data, and event records.

Benefits:

1. **Real-Time Data Processing**: Lambda functions allow IoT data to be processed in real-time, ensuring that the platform can immediately respond to changes or anomalies in the system.

2. **Scalability**: As the number of devices increases, the serverless architecture automatically scales to accommodate the additional load. This ensures that the system can handle data from thousands of devices without manual intervention.

3. **Cost-Effective**: With serverless computing, the IoT platform only pays for the actual data processing and functions executed, reducing infrastructure costs.

4. **Flexibility**: The event-driven nature of the system allows the platform to easily integrate new devices and handle new data streams without requiring significant changes to the architecture.

Challenges:

- **Data Consistency**: IoT data is often streamed in high volumes, and ensuring consistency between devices, data storage, and actions is critical. Using event-sourcing and CQRS patterns helps manage eventual consistency and improve performance.
- **Security**: Securing IoT devices and ensuring that the data transmitted between devices and the cloud is encrypted is a key concern. AWS IoT Core helps with secure communication and device management, but additional measures such as device authentication and role-based access control are necessary to ensure system security.

These case studies demonstrate the versatility and power of serverless architectures in various industries, from e-commerce to finance and IoT. By leveraging serverless microservices, organizations can scale more effectively, reduce operational overhead, and build highly resilient systems that can handle a wide range of use cases.

7.4 Case Study 4: Implementing CQRS in a Serverless Environment

The **CQRS (Command Query Responsibility Segregation)** pattern is particularly useful in complex systems where different aspects of the application require different data access patterns. In a serverless environment, applying CQRS enables optimization for both read and write operations. A common real-world use case for CQRS in a serverless environment is an order processing system for an e-commerce platform.

Scenario: Consider an e-commerce platform that needs to handle large volumes of customer orders. These orders need to be processed (commands), and the data needs to be queried frequently to show the current order status (queries). Using the CQRS pattern allows the platform to separate these two concerns, making each optimized for its specific purpose.

Serverless CQRS Components:

1. **Command Side (Write Operations)**: The write side is responsible for processing commands like creating, updating, and deleting data. These operations are handled by **AWS Lambda** functions triggered by events such as HTTP requests from customers or internal systems. The write operations update the data in a **DynamoDB table**.

2. **Query Side (Read Operations)**: The read side is optimized for querying the data, often for real-time retrieval of order information. Since queries can be read-heavy, the data model for reads is designed to be optimized for performance, possibly using denormalized data or read replicas of the original table. **Amazon DynamoDB** is used for fast, consistent reads, while data replication can be managed with **AWS Lambda** to update the read database whenever changes occur in the write model.

3. **Event-Driven Architecture**:
   - **AWS Lambda** functions handle the business logic for both the command and query sides.
   - **Amazon SNS** or **SQS** are used to trigger the propagation of events between the write and read models, ensuring eventual consistency between the two.

Benefits:

1. **Performance Optimization**: By decoupling the write and read operations, the system can optimize each for its specific use case. For example, the write model can focus on consistency and durability, while the read model is optimized for fast access.

2. **Scalability**: In serverless, the system automatically scales based on the workload. Read and write operations can scale independently, handling large spikes in customer orders or frequent lookups without impacting performance.

3. **Cost Efficiency**: Serverless functions only incur costs when executed, and the serverless environment handles scaling automatically, reducing the need for costly infrastructure maintenance.

Challenges:

1. **Eventual Consistency**: The primary challenge of CQRS is ensuring data consistency between the write and read models. In a serverless environment, maintaining eventual consistency requires careful event management and monitoring to ensure the system operates smoothly.
2. **Data Duplication**: The read model might require duplication of data to optimize query performance, which can lead to complications when the data in the write model changes.

By implementing CQRS in a serverless environment, this e-commerce platform can handle high volumes of orders efficiently and scale independently based on read or write demand.

7.5 Lessons Learned from Real-World Serverless Deployments

Real-world serverless deployments provide valuable lessons that can guide future implementations. These lessons reflect the challenges and benefits of working with serverless architectures and can help organizations optimize their use of serverless technologies.

1. Start Small and Iterate

When transitioning to serverless, it's crucial to start small. Many organizations attempt to migrate large, monolithic applications to serverless without fully understanding the limitations and potential challenges. Instead, begin by implementing serverless for specific use cases, such as microservices or individual components, and then gradually expand.

- **Example**: A company that tried to move their entire user authentication system to AWS Lambda in one go faced unforeseen issues like cold starts and limited resources, which impacted performance. By migrating the system incrementally, they were able to optimize each function for scalability and reliability.

2. Monitoring and Observability are Key

Serverless applications often involve multiple, decoupled services, making traditional monitoring tools ineffective. Implementing robust monitoring and observability tools is critical for identifying and resolving issues quickly.

- **Example**: A logistics company found it difficult to track function execution times and failures, leading to performance bottlenecks. By implementing **AWS CloudWatch**, they were able to identify slow Lambda functions, optimize them, and monitor event-driven workflows across multiple services.

3. Manage State Carefully

In serverless environments, functions are stateless by nature. However, many applications require maintaining state. Managing state in serverless can be tricky because it often requires external storage solutions, such as databases or object storage, which can introduce latency.

- **Example**: An IoT company experienced issues when trying to maintain session state in a stateless serverless application. They addressed this by integrating **AWS DynamoDB** with **AWS Lambda** to store state information persistently and reduce the overhead of managing state externally.

4. Understand Cost Implications

While serverless offers cost efficiency due to its pay-per-use model, it's important to understand how costs scale with traffic. High-function invocation rates can lead to increased costs, especially when Lambda functions interact with external services like databases or APIs.

- **Example**: A social media company saw unexpected cost spikes when they implemented Lambda for real-time image processing. After analyzing usage patterns, they optimized function invocations by introducing more efficient processing algorithms and reducing calls to external APIs.

5. Be Prepared for Cold Starts

Lambda cold starts can cause delays in function execution, particularly in high-throughput systems where low latency is crucial. Cold starts occur when a Lambda function is invoked after being idle for a period, causing it to initialize before execution.

- **Example**: A streaming platform experienced delays during user authentication due to Lambda cold starts. They mitigated this issue by using **AWS Lambda Provisioned Concurrency**, which keeps a specified number of function instances warm, reducing cold start times.

7.6 Analyzing Failures: What Went Wrong in Real-World Serverless Systems?

Despite its advantages, serverless computing has its challenges, and failures are inevitable. Analyzing these failures is crucial for understanding what went wrong and improving system reliability in future implementations.

1. Inconsistent Data Synchronization

In event-driven architectures, where data is passed between different services via events, ensuring data consistency can be a challenge. If an event is lost or not processed correctly, it can lead to inconsistent data states across services.

- **Failure Example**: An e-commerce company faced issues with inventory synchronization between the payment service and the stock management system. After a failed event, the stock count was not updated, leading to overselling. The solution involved adding dead-letter queues and retry mechanisms to ensure that failed events were handled correctly.

2. Resource Limitations

Lambda functions are constrained by resource limits, such as execution time, memory, and network bandwidth. These limitations can cause unexpected failures if the resources allocated to a function are insufficient for the tasks it performs.

- **Failure Example**: A video transcoding service using AWS Lambda failed to process larger video files because the functions were constrained by the default memory and timeout settings. The issue was resolved by adjusting the memory allocation and increasing the timeout limit for specific Lambda functions.

3. Lack of Proper Monitoring and Alerts

Serverless applications can be difficult to monitor due to their distributed and dynamic nature. Without proper monitoring tools, it can be challenging to identify the root cause of a failure or pinpoint underperforming services.

- **Failure Example**: A financial company faced delays in processing transactions due to a misconfigured Lambda function that wasn't being logged properly. By implementing a more comprehensive monitoring solution, including **AWS X-Ray** for distributed tracing and **CloudWatch Logs** for logging, they were able to identify and resolve issues quickly.

4. Security Vulnerabilities

With serverless applications, managing security can be complex. Each Lambda function has its own access permissions, and improperly configured IAM roles or missing authorization checks can expose vulnerabilities.

- **Failure Example**: A healthcare provider accidentally exposed sensitive user data due to improper IAM role permissions. After conducting a thorough security audit, they implemented tighter IAM policies and ensured that all Lambda functions used the principle of least privilege.

5. Cold Start Delays

In certain real-time applications, Lambda cold starts can introduce delays that disrupt the user experience. While AWS has optimized cold start times over the years, certain use cases still experience latency due to cold starts.

- **Failure Example**: A ride-sharing platform saw increased latency in ride request processing during off-peak hours due to Lambda cold starts. The solution involved using **Lambda Provisioned Concurrency** to pre-warm certain critical functions during peak hours, reducing cold start impact.

7.7 Best Practices for Serverless Microservices Implementations

To ensure successful serverless microservices deployments, certain best practices should be followed. These practices will help streamline development, improve reliability, and optimize the performance of serverless applications.

1. Design for Failure

In serverless systems, failure is inevitable. Design your system to handle failures gracefully by implementing retry mechanisms, dead-letter queues, and fallback strategies. Ensure that services can recover from errors without causing cascading failures.

2. Use Event-Driven Architectures

Serverless is naturally suited for event-driven architectures. Use events to decouple services and allow them to operate asynchronously. This ensures that services are loosely coupled, making the system more scalable and fault-tolerant.

3. Optimize Cold Starts

Cold starts can impact the performance of serverless functions, particularly for latency-sensitive applications. To mitigate cold starts, use techniques like **Lambda Provisioned Concurrency** to pre-warm functions that require low latency.

4. Monitor and Log Everything

Use monitoring tools like **AWS CloudWatch** and **AWS X-Ray** to monitor serverless functions and track metrics such as invocation count, duration, and error rates. Ensure comprehensive logging to help diagnose issues and improve performance.

5. Apply the Principle of Least Privilege

When setting IAM roles and policies, always follow the principle of least privilege. Only grant the necessary permissions for each Lambda function to perform its job. This minimizes security risks and reduces the attack surface.

6. Use Infrastructure as Code (IaC)

Adopt Infrastructure as Code (IaC) to manage and provision serverless resources. Tools like the **Serverless Framework**, **AWS CloudFormation**, and **Terraform** allow you to define, deploy, and manage serverless infrastructure in a repeatable and consistent manner.

7. Test Locally and Continuously

Before deploying serverless functions to production, thoroughly test them locally using tools like **Serverless Offline** or **LocalStack**. Implement continuous testing and integration pipelines to automate testing and ensure the quality of your serverless code.

By following these best practices, you can ensure that your serverless microservices are efficient, reliable, and secure, leading to better performance and a smoother user experience.

This chapter covered various real-world applications of serverless architectures and provided valuable insights into the benefits, challenges, and best practices for implementing serverless microservices. These case studies offer practical examples that help understand how serverless systems can be optimized for real-world use cases.

Chapter 8: Testing, Debugging, and Monitoring Serverless Microservices

8.1 Testing Serverless Functions: Approaches and Tools

Testing serverless functions is often more challenging than traditional server-based applications because of the distributed nature of serverless systems and the limited local execution environment. However, effective testing is crucial for ensuring that serverless microservices work reliably and efficiently.

Approaches to Testing Serverless Functions:

1. **Unit Testing**

   Unit testing in serverless architectures involves testing individual functions in isolation, independent of external services or dependencies. The goal is to verify that the function behaves correctly for a given input and produces the expected output.

   - **Mocking External Dependencies**: In serverless applications, functions often interact with external services such as databases (DynamoDB, RDS), APIs (REST, GraphQL), and messaging systems (SNS, SQS). To unit test serverless functions, external dependencies can be mocked using libraries like **Jest**, **Mocha**, or **Sinon**. These mock libraries allow developers to simulate the behavior of AWS services, enabling them to test Lambda functions locally without actually interacting with the cloud.
   - **Example**: Using **AWS SDK Mock** to mock AWS service calls allows unit tests to simulate interactions with DynamoDB or S3 while avoiding external dependencies.

javascript

Copy

```javascript
const AWS = require('aws-sdk-mock');
const handler = require('./handler');

test('Lambda function successfully processes data', async () => {
  AWS.mock('DynamoDB.DocumentClient', 'put', Promise.resolve());

  const event = { body: '{"userId": "123", "orderId": "456"}' };
  const response = await handler.createOrder(event);

  expect(response.statusCode).toBe(200);
  AWS.restore('DynamoDB.DocumentClient');
});
```

2. **Local Testing**

   Local testing allows developers to test serverless functions on their local machine before deploying them to the cloud. This is essential for early-stage development and debugging.

   - **Serverless Framework**: The **Serverless Framework** offers a local testing plugin, **serverless-offline**, that allows Lambda functions to be run locally by simulating API Gateway and Lambda events. This provides a way to test serverless functions without needing to deploy them to the cloud each time.
   - **LocalStack**: **LocalStack** is a popular tool that simulates AWS services locally, providing an environment where serverless functions can be tested before deployment. This tool allows developers to test Lambda functions, DynamoDB, S3, and other AWS services on their local machine.

117

Example of testing with **serverless-offline**:

bash

Copy

serverless offline start

3. This command starts an API Gateway locally, enabling you to invoke Lambda functions on your local machine by hitting the defined endpoints.

4. **End-to-End (E2E) Testing**

E2E testing simulates user interactions and tests the serverless application as a whole. E2E tests are typically run in staging environments where the full serverless stack, including API Gateway, Lambda, DynamoDB, etc., is deployed. Tools like **Cypress**, **Puppeteer**, or **Selenium** can be used for simulating HTTP requests to the API and verifying that the functions integrate correctly across services.

   o **Example**: Testing the full flow of a user login process by sending requests to an API Gateway endpoint and verifying the responses and database state.

javascript

Copy

```javascript
describe('User Login E2E Test', () => {
  it('should successfully log in a user', () => {
    cy.request('POST', 'https://api.example.com/login', {
      username: 'testuser',
      password: 'password123',
    }).then((response) => {
      expect(response.status).to.eq(200);
      expect(response.body).to.have.property('message', 'Login successful');
    });
  });
});
```

118

5. **Tools for Testing Serverless Functions**:

- **Jest**: A widely-used JavaScript testing framework for unit tests and mocks.
- **Mocha**: A flexible test framework often used in Node.js applications, alongside **Chai** for assertions.
- **AWS SDK Mock**: A library to mock AWS SDK calls for unit testing serverless functions.
- **serverless-offline**: A plugin for the Serverless Framework that allows local simulation of AWS services.
- **LocalStack**: A fully functional local AWS cloud stack for local testing of serverless applications.

8.2 Unit Testing and Integration Testing in Serverless Applications

Testing serverless applications requires both unit testing individual functions and integration testing the interactions between these functions and external services. Here, we will break down both types of testing and the tools used to implement them.

1. Unit Testing in Serverless

Unit testing in serverless applications focuses on testing individual Lambda functions in isolation. For a unit test to be effective, it should mock dependencies, simulate inputs, and verify that the Lambda function produces the expected results.

- **Mocking Dependencies**: Serverless functions interact with external resources such as databases, APIs, and messaging systems. These interactions can be mocked to isolate the unit being tested.
- **Test Coverage**: Unit tests should cover the core business logic of the function, ensuring that it handles different input scenarios correctly. Common scenarios to test include:
    - Valid and invalid inputs.
    - Error handling for missing data or failed interactions with external services.

Example of a Unit Test for AWS Lambda:

javascript

Copy

```javascript
const AWS = require('aws-sdk-mock');
const handler = require('./handler'); // Lambda function handler

describe('Create Order Lambda', () => {
  it('should create an order successfully', async () => {
    AWS.mock('DynamoDB.DocumentClient', 'put', Promise.resolve());

    const event = {
      body: '{"userId":"123", "orderId":"456", "total":100}'
    };

    const response = await handler.createOrder(event);

    expect(response.statusCode).toBe(200);
    expect(JSON.parse(response.body).message).toBe('Order created successfully');
    AWS.restore('DynamoDB.DocumentClient');
  });

  it('should return an error for missing data', async () => {
    const event = { body: '{}' }; // Missing required fields

    const response = await handler.createOrder(event);

    expect(response.statusCode).toBe(400);
    expect(JSON.parse(response.body).message).toBe('Invalid input');
  });
```

120

```
});
```

2. Integration Testing in Serverless

Integration testing verifies that individual components of the serverless system interact correctly. This includes testing Lambda functions with actual external services like DynamoDB, API Gateway, or S3.

- **Setting Up Integration Tests**: Integration tests should test the function end-to-end, interacting with the actual cloud resources (although in some cases, services like **LocalStack** or **DynamoDB Local** can be used to simulate the cloud environment locally).
- **Validating Data Flow**: Ensure that the Lambda function properly interacts with external systems (e.g., stores data in DynamoDB, triggers SNS notifications, or sends data to S3).

Example of Integration Test for Serverless Application:

javascript

Copy

```javascript
const AWS = require('aws-sdk');
const dynamoDB = new AWS.DynamoDB.DocumentClient();
const handler = require('./handler'); // Lambda function handler

describe('Create User Integration Test', () => {
  it('should create a user in DynamoDB', async () => {
    const event = {
      body: '{"userId":"123", "name":"John Doe"}'
    };

    const response = await handler.createUser(event);
```

```javascript
expect(response.statusCode).toBe(200);
expect(JSON.parse(response.body).message).toBe('User created successfully');

// Validate the entry in DynamoDB
const params = {
  TableName: 'Users',
  Key: {
    userId: '123'
  }
};

const result = await dynamoDB.get(params).promise();
expect(result.Item).toBeDefined();
expect(result.Item.name).toBe('John Doe');
});
});
```

3. Best Practices for Testing Serverless Applications:

- **Use Mocks**: Mock external dependencies, especially for unit tests, to avoid making real network calls.
- **Test in Isolation**: Unit tests should test individual Lambda functions without depending on other components.
- **Test with Real Data**: For integration tests, ensure that the tests interact with real services (or local replicas) to validate the full flow.
- **Run Tests Locally**: Use tools like **serverless-offline** and **LocalStack** to run serverless functions locally, enabling faster feedback during development.

8.3 Automated Testing Pipelines for Serverless Deployments

Automating the testing of serverless applications through continuous integration (CI) and continuous deployment (CD) pipelines is essential for maintaining the quality of the system and ensuring reliable releases.

1. Setting Up a CI/CD Pipeline

CI/CD pipelines automate the process of testing, building, and deploying serverless applications. This ensures that code changes are automatically tested before being deployed to production.

- **Popular CI/CD Tools for Serverless**:
  - **GitHub Actions**: GitHub Actions is an excellent choice for automating testing and deployment in serverless applications, offering seamless integration with AWS and other services.
  - **CircleCI**: CircleCI is another popular tool that can automate testing and deployment pipelines for serverless applications, with built-in support for Docker, AWS Lambda, and other serverless resources.
  - **AWS CodePipeline**: AWS's native CI/CD tool that integrates directly with services like Lambda, API Gateway, and DynamoDB.

2. Example CI/CD Pipeline with GitHub Actions

Here's an example of how you can set up a basic **GitHub Actions** pipeline to deploy a serverless application:

yaml

Copy

```
name: Deploy Serverless Application

on:
  push:
    branches:
```

```yaml
      - main

jobs:
  deploy:
    runs-on: ubuntu-latest
    steps:
      - name: Checkout code
        uses: actions/checkout@v2

      - name: Set up Node.js
        uses: actions/setup-node@v2
        with:
          node-version: '14'

      - name: Install dependencies
        run: npm install

      - name: Run tests
        run: npm test

      - name: Deploy to AWS Lambda
        run: npx serverless deploy --stage prod
        env:
          AWS_ACCESS_KEY_ID: ${{ secrets.AWS_ACCESS_KEY_ID }}
          AWS_SECRET_ACCESS_KEY: ${{ secrets.AWS_SECRET_ACCESS_KEY }}
          AWS_REGION: ${{ secrets.AWS_REGION }}
```

This pipeline:

1. Runs when changes are pushed to the main branch.
2. Checks out the code from the repository.
3. Sets up Node.js and installs dependencies.
4. Runs tests before deployment.
5. Deploys the serverless application to AWS Lambda using the **Serverless Framework**.

3. Automated Tests in CI/CD Pipelines:

- **Unit Tests**: Run unit tests during the build phase to validate that individual functions work correctly.
- **Integration Tests**: Run integration tests in staging or testing environments to validate that services interact correctly.
- **Performance Tests**: Test the performance of Lambda functions to ensure that they meet latency and throughput requirements.
- **End-to-End Tests**: Run end-to-end tests to ensure that the entire system works as expected in a real-world scenario.

4. Continuous Deployment:

- Set up the pipeline to automatically deploy the serverless application after successful tests. Tools like **AWS CodePipeline**, **Serverless Framework**, and **GitHub Actions** support automatic deployment to production after tests pass.

Best Practices for Automated Testing Pipelines:

- **Use Multiple Environments**: Set up separate environments for development, staging, and production to test serverless applications thoroughly before deploying to live systems.
- **Fail Fast**: Ensure the pipeline fails as soon as a test fails to prevent faulty code from being deployed.

- **Clean Up Resources**: Implement resource cleanup mechanisms in your CI/CD pipeline to avoid running up unnecessary costs in the cloud after each test or deployment.

By integrating automated testing into your CI/CD pipeline, you can ensure that your serverless application is continuously tested, validated, and deployed in a reliable and efficient manner.

We covered the best approaches and tools for testing, debugging, and monitoring serverless microservices. By applying these techniques, developers can ensure that serverless functions operate smoothly and meet performance, reliability, and scalability requirements. Testing serverless functions locally, automating test pipelines, and implementing robust monitoring are essential steps in maintaining the quality of serverless applications.

8.4 Debugging Serverless Architectures: Techniques and Tools

Debugging serverless architectures presents unique challenges due to the stateless nature of serverless functions, the distributed environment, and the lack of direct access to the underlying infrastructure. However, by using the right techniques and tools, you can effectively debug serverless applications to identify and resolve issues quickly.

1. Local Debugging with Serverless Framework

One of the first steps in debugging serverless applications is to test functions locally before deploying them to the cloud. Tools like **serverless-offline** and **LocalStack** allow you to emulate AWS services locally, helping you debug Lambda functions without making live API calls.

Serverless Offline Plugin: This plugin simulates API Gateway and Lambda events locally, allowing you to test functions as though they are running on AWS. It also supports local invocation of events like HTTP requests, SNS events, and DynamoDB

126

triggers.

Example:

bash

Copy

serverless offline start

- **LocalStack**: LocalStack is a tool that simulates AWS services locally, allowing you to test Lambda functions, DynamoDB, S3, and other AWS services in a local environment.

    Example:

    bash

    Copy

    docker run -d -p 4566:4566 localstack/localstack

2. Remote Debugging and Cloud Debuggers

For remote debugging in a cloud environment, use AWS CloudWatch Logs and AWS X-Ray. While traditional debuggers are limited in serverless environments, cloud-based tools help track and analyze Lambda function executions and identify performance bottlenecks or errors.

- **CloudWatch Logs**: AWS CloudWatch Logs can capture detailed logs for Lambda functions, which you can analyze to understand what happened before a failure occurred.
    - Use **console.log()** or **console.error()** statements within your Lambda functions to capture logs that can be analyzed in CloudWatch Logs.
    - Use CloudWatch Insights to search logs for errors and performance issues, making it easier to identify patterns across Lambda executions.
- **AWS X-Ray**: AWS X-Ray provides distributed tracing for Lambda functions and other AWS resources, enabling you to trace requests as they pass through multiple services in a serverless application.

127

- X-Ray helps identify performance bottlenecks, service latencies, and issues such as failed invocations or slow executions.

3. Debugging Cold Starts

Cold starts can introduce delays in serverless applications, especially when functions are not invoked for a while. To debug cold starts, monitor Lambda function durations and analyze cold start times in AWS CloudWatch Metrics. Reduce cold start latency by optimizing Lambda functions for faster initialization or using **Lambda Provisioned Concurrency**.

4. Debugging AWS Lambda Function Errors

When debugging Lambda functions, consider the following common error types:

- **Timeouts**: Functions that run for longer than the configured timeout limit will fail. Increase the timeout duration in the Lambda function configuration, or optimize the function code for performance.
- **Memory Exhaustion**: If a Lambda function exceeds its memory allocation, it will fail. Increase the memory limit or optimize the function's memory usage.
- **Missing Environment Variables**: Ensure all necessary environment variables are correctly set for your Lambda function.

5. Using CloudWatch Alarms for Debugging

Set up CloudWatch Alarms to track function errors, high latency, or excessive invocations. These alarms can notify you when issues occur, helping you identify problems quickly.

6. Testing with Mock Data

To reproduce bugs or issues locally, test your functions using mock data that simulates real-world inputs. Tools like **Jest** or **Mocha** can help create mock versions of AWS SDKs or other external dependencies that Lambda functions rely on.

8.5 Monitoring Serverless Applications: Tools for Observability

Serverless applications require robust monitoring and observability to ensure they are running smoothly. Since serverless functions are distributed across multiple services and do not have a persistent state, effective monitoring tools can help track performance, diagnose issues, and ensure reliability.

1. AWS CloudWatch

AWS CloudWatch is the primary monitoring and observability tool for AWS serverless applications. It provides a wide range of features, including metrics, logs, alarms, and dashboards, to monitor the health and performance of Lambda functions, API Gateway, DynamoDB, and other AWS services.

- **CloudWatch Metrics**: Lambda functions send performance metrics such as invocation count, duration, errors, and cold starts to CloudWatch, which can be used to monitor performance and set alarms.
- **CloudWatch Logs**: CloudWatch Logs capture detailed logs from Lambda functions. Use logs to debug issues, trace execution flows, and monitor the behavior of functions in real time.
- **CloudWatch Dashboards**: Use CloudWatch Dashboards to create custom visualizations for your serverless application. Dashboards allow you to track key metrics across multiple services and functions.

2. AWS X-Ray for Distributed Tracing

AWS X-Ray helps with **distributed tracing** by tracking requests as they flow through multiple services, such as Lambda, API Gateway, DynamoDB, and others. X-Ray can help identify bottlenecks, errors, and performance issues across the entire application.

- **X-Ray Integration**: Enable X-Ray for your Lambda functions by configuring it in the Lambda console or using the AWS SDK. You can also track specific segments of your application, such as requests to DynamoDB or API Gateway.

129

- **X-Ray Insights**: X-Ray Insights automatically analyzes trace data to highlight unusual patterns, such as high latencies, errors, or resource bottlenecks.

3. Third-Party Monitoring Tools

Third-party monitoring and observability tools can complement AWS-native solutions by offering more granular insights, advanced analytics, and multi-cloud compatibility. Popular third-party tools include:

- **Datadog**: A monitoring and observability platform that integrates with AWS services to provide real-time metrics, traces, and logs for Lambda and other serverless resources.
- **New Relic**: A performance monitoring platform that provides serverless-specific features, including Lambda monitoring, error tracking, and performance optimization.
- **Sentry**: An error monitoring tool that integrates with AWS Lambda to capture and report errors in serverless functions.

4. Metrics and Dashboards

Create custom dashboards using CloudWatch or third-party tools to track key performance indicators (KPIs) for your serverless functions:

- **Invocation Rate**: Track how many times Lambda functions are invoked, and monitor traffic spikes.
- **Error Rate**: Monitor the percentage of failed invocations and identify the root cause of errors.
- **Duration**: Monitor Lambda execution times to identify performance bottlenecks.
- **Cold Starts**: Track cold starts to optimize Lambda functions and minimize delays.

5. Alerting and Notifications

Set up CloudWatch Alarms or third-party alerts to notify you when specific conditions are met, such as high error rates, slow performance, or resource exhaustion. Alerts can be sent via email, SMS, or integrated with tools like **Slack** or **PagerDuty** for real-time notifications.

8.6 Distributed Tracing in Serverless Microservices

Distributed tracing is essential for understanding the flow of requests across multiple serverless functions and services in a microservices architecture. By using distributed tracing, developers can track requests across different Lambda functions, identify performance bottlenecks, and monitor inter-service communication.

1. Introduction to Distributed Tracing

Distributed tracing allows you to track requests as they travel through various microservices, making it easier to visualize the flow of data. In a serverless architecture, requests often trigger multiple Lambda functions, each interacting with various AWS services (DynamoDB, SQS, SNS, etc.). Tracing helps you understand how these functions interact and where performance issues or errors might occur.

2. AWS X-Ray for Distributed Tracing

AWS X-Ray is the most common tool for distributed tracing in AWS serverless applications. It automatically collects trace data for Lambda functions and other AWS services.

- **X-Ray Trace Data**: X-Ray captures detailed trace data for each request, including function execution time, the status of interactions with other services (e.g., DynamoDB queries), and potential error details.
- **Service Map**: X-Ray provides a service map that visualizes the interactions between Lambda functions, databases, and other AWS services. This helps pinpoint the source of performance issues and errors in the system.

3. Tracing Lambda Function Calls

To enable tracing for AWS Lambda functions, simply enable **X-Ray** tracing in the

Lambda console or via the AWS SDK. For example, you can enable tracing in the Serverless Framework by adding the following to your serverless.yml file:

yaml

Copy

```yaml
functions:
  myFunction:
    handler: handler.myFunction
    tracing: Active
```

This configuration sends trace data to X-Ray, where you can view detailed performance metrics and logs.

4. Benefits of Distributed Tracing

- **End-to-End Visibility**: Track the flow of requests from start to finish across multiple Lambda functions and services.
- **Identify Bottlenecks**: Pinpoint where requests are delayed, whether in Lambda execution, external service calls, or inter-service communication.
- **Optimize Performance**: Use trace data to identify underperforming Lambda functions, long-running tasks, or inefficient service interactions.

5. Integration with Third-Party Tools

AWS X-Ray can integrate with third-party tools like **Datadog** and **New Relic** to enhance your tracing capabilities. These tools provide advanced analytics, additional visualizations, and unified dashboards for your serverless applications.

8.7 Error Handling and Logging in Serverless Environments

Error handling and logging are crucial for debugging and monitoring serverless applications. In serverless environments, Lambda functions may fail due to a variety of reasons, such as incorrect input, service unavailability, or timeouts. Effective error handling ensures that functions fail gracefully, and proper logging helps you identify and resolve issues quickly.

1. Lambda Error Handling

AWS Lambda provides several mechanisms for handling errors and failures:

- **Retries**: Lambda automatically retries failed invocations for certain event sources (e.g., SQS, SNS) based on the retry configuration.

Dead Letter Queues (DLQ): For functions that fail repeatedly, you can configure a **Dead Letter Queue** to store failed events for later processing or debugging.
Example configuration in serverless.yml:
yaml
Copy

```
functions:

  myFunction:

    handler: handler.myFunction

    deadLetter:

      targetArn: arn:aws:sqs:region:account-id:dlq
```

2. Logging with CloudWatch Logs

Logging is a fundamental part of debugging and understanding the behavior of Lambda functions. Lambda automatically integrates with **CloudWatch Logs** to capture execution logs.

- **Console Logs**: Use console.log(), console.error(), and other logging functions in your Lambda code to log important information. These logs will appear in CloudWatch Logs, where you can review them for error details.

Structured Logs: Consider logging structured data (e.g., JSON) to make it easier to parse and analyze logs. For example:

javascript

Copy

```
console.log(JSON.stringify({ event, status: 'processing', timestamp: new Date() }));
```

3. Error Monitoring

To identify and respond to errors quickly, use error monitoring tools such as:

- **Sentry**: An open-source error tracking tool that captures errors and performance issues from Lambda functions, giving you visibility into production errors.
- **Datadog**: A monitoring tool that provides enhanced logging, error reporting, and anomaly detection for serverless functions.

4. Handling Asynchronous Errors

In event-driven architectures, errors can occur in asynchronous workflows (e.g., message processing with SQS or SNS). Ensure that:

- Errors are logged in CloudWatch.
- Use DLQs for unprocessed events or failed invocations to reprocess them later.
- Integrate with alerting tools like **SNS** to notify the team when critical errors occur.

5. Best Practices for Error Handling and Logging:

- Always include detailed error messages in logs, including relevant context like input parameters, environment variables, and timeouts.
- Implement robust retry and fallback strategies to recover from transient failures.

- Use **DLQs** to isolate and manage failed events, preventing them from affecting the main processing workflow.
- Set up **CloudWatch Alarms** to alert your team about specific errors or failure rates that exceed thresholds.

This chapter highlighted essential techniques for debugging, monitoring, and ensuring observability in serverless microservices applications. By leveraging tools like **AWS CloudWatch**, **AWS X-Ray**, and third-party platforms, you can enhance your ability to track function execution, diagnose performance issues, and maintain a stable, resilient serverless environment.

Chapter 9: Performance Optimization and Cost Management

9.1 Optimizing Function Performance in Serverless Architectures

Performance optimization in serverless applications is crucial for ensuring fast response times, efficient resource usage, and the scalability of your application. In serverless architectures, each function is designed to be lightweight and isolated, but they can still experience performance bottlenecks due to inefficient code, resource limitations, or poor design patterns. Let's explore strategies for optimizing function performance in a serverless environment.

1. Code Optimization The first step in optimizing Lambda function performance is to ensure that the code itself is efficient. Here are some techniques to improve code performance:

- **Minimize Initialization Time**: Lambda functions have an initialization phase during which resources are allocated and the code is loaded. To minimize this phase, keep your functions small and modular. Avoid loading large dependencies or performing unnecessary setup tasks.
- **Use Efficient Libraries**: Be mindful of the libraries and frameworks you use in your Lambda functions. Heavy or bloated libraries can increase function startup time. Consider using lighter alternatives or only importing necessary modules.
- **Optimize Loops and Logic**: Optimize loops, recursion, and logic in your function. Ensure that loops are as efficient as possible, avoid deep recursion that could lead to stack overflows, and minimize the complexity of your function logic.

2. Use of Concurrency and Parallelism AWS Lambda functions are inherently parallel, meaning they can handle multiple requests simultaneously. However, you can further optimize performance by making use of concurrency.

- **Reserve Concurrency**: For critical functions, consider reserving concurrency, ensuring that the function is always available to handle requests. Reserved concurrency guarantees that a specific number of function instances are always available, preventing scaling delays during traffic spikes.
- **Use Parallel Processing**: For functions that process large volumes of data (e.g., batch jobs or large file uploads), consider breaking the data into smaller chunks and processing them in parallel. Use AWS services like **SQS** or **SNS** to trigger multiple Lambda functions concurrently.

3. Reducing Function Size Lambda functions with large deployment packages or dependencies can experience longer cold starts, which can negatively impact performance. To reduce function size:

- **Use Layers**: AWS Lambda Layers allow you to package and share libraries or dependencies separately from the function code. By separating reusable components (e.g., third-party libraries) into layers, you reduce the overall size of your function code.
- **Minify Code**: Minify your function code to remove unnecessary whitespace, comments, and unused code. This can significantly reduce the deployment package size, especially for JavaScript or Python-based functions.

4. Memory Allocation Memory plays a critical role in Lambda function performance. By adjusting the memory allocation, you can affect both performance and cost:

- **Fine-Tune Memory Settings**: AWS Lambda automatically allocates CPU power in proportion to the memory you assign. Functions with higher memory allocations run faster because they have more processing power. However, this

137

also increases the cost. Test different memory configurations to find the balance between speed and cost.

- **Monitor Memory Usage**: Use CloudWatch to monitor memory usage and function duration. If your function frequently uses close to its allocated memory, it may be worth increasing the allocation to optimize performance.

5. Efficient Use of External Services Serverless functions often interact with external services like databases, APIs, and storage systems. Optimizing these interactions is key to improving overall performance.

- **Batch Database Operations**: When working with databases like DynamoDB or RDS, batch multiple database operations (e.g., inserts, updates, queries) into a single request to reduce the number of calls made to the database.
- **Use Caching**: Cache frequently accessed data in-memory or in a caching layer (e.g., **Amazon ElastiCache**, **AWS DynamoDB Accelerator (DAX)**) to reduce latency and avoid repeated queries to external systems.

9.2 Managing Serverless Function Execution Time

Serverless function execution time has a direct impact on both performance and cost. AWS Lambda charges you based on the execution time, so optimizing the time a function spends processing a request is crucial for both speed and cost-effectiveness.

1. Shorten Function Execution Time To reduce execution time, focus on optimizing the function's internal logic and external interactions:

- **Optimize Dependencies**: Only import the necessary parts of libraries or frameworks to keep the initialization time short. Use asynchronous programming techniques to ensure that I/O operations do not block other tasks.
- **Use Asynchronous Operations**: If your function involves I/O-bound tasks (e.g., reading from a database or an API), consider making the operations

asynchronous. This allows the function to handle other tasks while waiting for I/O operations to complete.

- **Avoid Unnecessary Waits**: Minimize the use of waiting or sleeping functions, as they unnecessarily extend execution time. If you need to wait for a response from a downstream service, use non-blocking calls, such as **async/await** or **Promise** in JavaScript, or equivalent constructs in other languages.

2. Reduce Cold Start Time Cold starts occur when a Lambda function is invoked for the first time or after it has been idle for a period. While AWS Lambda has significantly reduced cold start latency, it can still be a concern in high-performance applications.

- **Use Lambda Provisioned Concurrency**: **Provisioned Concurrency** keeps a specific number of Lambda instances warm and ready to handle requests, eliminating cold start delays. This is especially useful for latency-sensitive applications, such as real-time APIs or customer-facing applications.
- **Keep Functions Warm**: For functions that need to stay warm between invocations, set up a simple Lambda function or scheduled event (via **AWS CloudWatch Events**) that calls your function periodically to prevent it from going idle.

3. Optimize External Dependencies When interacting with external services, such as databases, APIs, or message queues, minimize the latency of these interactions.

- **Optimize Database Queries**: Ensure that database queries are efficient by using proper indexes, query optimizations, and avoiding expensive operations like full table scans.
- **Use Connection Pools**: Instead of opening new database connections for each request, use connection pooling to reuse connections, which significantly reduces latency for database operations.

9.3 Reducing Latency in Serverless Systems

Latency in serverless systems can arise from multiple sources, including cold starts, network delays, and inefficient service interactions. Minimizing latency is crucial for ensuring a fast user experience.

1. Reduce Cold Start Latency Cold starts can introduce significant delays in serverless functions, especially if they are invoked infrequently or with large dependencies. Reducing cold start latency involves the following:

- **Provisioned Concurrency**: As mentioned earlier, provisioned concurrency ensures that your Lambda functions are pre-warmed and available for immediate invocation, reducing cold start times significantly.
- **Reduce the Size of the Deployment Package**: Smaller Lambda function packages result in faster initialization times, as less code needs to be loaded into memory.
- **Use Lighter Runtimes**: Some runtimes, such as **Node.js** or **Go**, tend to have faster cold start times compared to others like **Java**. Choose the runtime based on your application's needs and performance benchmarks.

2. Minimize Network Latency Network latency can be a significant bottleneck, especially when Lambda functions are interacting with remote services or APIs.

- **Use Regional Resources**: Deploy Lambda functions and other services (e.g., DynamoDB, S3) in the same AWS region to reduce network latency.
- **Leverage VPC Connectivity**: If your Lambda functions need to access resources inside a Virtual Private Cloud (VPC), make sure the Lambda function is optimized for VPC access. AWS provides VPC networking enhancements, such as **VPC endpoints** and **AWS Direct Connect**, that can help reduce latency.

3. Optimize Data Transfer When Lambda functions need to process large amounts of data, the time it takes to transfer this data can increase latency.

- **Use Streamlining Techniques**: When passing data between services (e.g., between Lambda and DynamoDB), make sure that the data is in the most efficient format (e.g., JSON, binary) and that unnecessary data is excluded.
- **Use SQS or SNS for Queueing**: For large data processing tasks, consider using SQS or SNS to buffer data, which allows the system to process smaller batches of data in parallel, reducing latency.

4. Implementing Edge Computing For latency-sensitive applications, such as those that require real-time processing, consider using **AWS Lambda@Edge**. Lambda@Edge allows you to run functions closer to the user, at AWS locations worldwide, which reduces latency by processing data closer to the end-user.

9.4 Cost Optimization in Serverless Applications

Cost management in serverless architectures is one of the most significant advantages of using serverless computing. However, it's important to understand how AWS Lambda's pricing works and implement strategies to ensure your application is cost-effective.

1. Optimize Function Execution Time AWS Lambda charges based on the duration of each function invocation. By optimizing function execution time, you can significantly reduce costs.

- **Optimize Code**: As mentioned earlier, optimizing the function code to minimize execution time and resource usage will directly reduce the time the function runs, lowering costs.
- **Monitor Execution Time**: Use CloudWatch to monitor function durations and identify any long-running functions that may need optimization.

2. Adjust Memory Allocation Lambda charges are based on both execution time and memory allocation. Allocating more memory allows your function to run faster but can increase costs. Therefore, it's essential to find a balance between memory allocation and execution time.

141

- **Test Different Memory Allocations**: Use CloudWatch metrics to experiment with different memory settings and find the optimal configuration for your functions.
- **Fine-Tune for Performance**: Allocate the least amount of memory necessary to meet performance goals. Excessive memory allocation leads to higher costs, while insufficient memory allocation leads to slower performance and longer execution times.

3. Use AWS Lambda's Free Tier AWS Lambda provides a free tier that includes 1 million free requests and 400,000 GB-seconds of compute time per month. If your application has low traffic or limited function invocations, you can take advantage of the free tier to reduce costs.

4. Control Function Frequency Each invocation of a Lambda function incurs costs. You can reduce costs by controlling how often your functions are invoked.

- **Event Filtering**: Use event filtering in services like SNS or SQS to ensure that Lambda functions are triggered only for relevant events.
- **Scheduled Events**: Use **CloudWatch Events** to schedule Lambda invocations only when necessary, rather than triggering them on every event.

5. Use Reserved Concurrency and Provisioned Concurrency For critical functions, you can reserve concurrency to ensure that the function always runs within its defined concurrency limit. This guarantees that the function is always available, but it can also result in higher costs.

- **Reserved Concurrency**: Use reserved concurrency to guarantee that your Lambda function always has the resources it needs to run.
- **Provisioned Concurrency**: Use provisioned concurrency to keep a set number of Lambda instances warm, reducing cold start latency, but be aware that this increases costs since you are paying for the warm instances.

6. Manage Data Transfer Costs In serverless systems, data transfer between services can result in additional costs. To reduce these costs:

- **Minimize Data Transfers**: Ensure that data is transferred between services as efficiently as possible. Avoid unnecessary data transfers or multiple hops between services.
- **Optimize API Calls**: Use batching or aggregation techniques to reduce the number of API calls made to external services, minimizing the associated data transfer costs.

9.5 Best Practices for Scaling Serverless Microservices

Serverless architectures are inherently scalable, but to fully realize their potential, you need to implement best practices to ensure your serverless microservices scale efficiently and cost-effectively. Here are some best practices for scaling serverless microservices:

1. Design Microservices for Independence One of the key principles of serverless microservices is that each service should be independent and perform a specific function. When scaling serverless applications, it's crucial that each microservice can scale independently based on demand. This ensures that you can allocate resources efficiently without affecting the entire system.

- **Avoid Tight Coupling**: Design each microservice to have its own data store, API, and logic, allowing them to scale without interference from other services.
- **Event-Driven Architecture**: Use an event-driven architecture where services respond to events (e.g., through SNS, SQS, or Kinesis). This ensures that services scale as needed without overloading others.

2. Implement Horizontal Scaling for Stateless Functions Lambda functions are stateless, which means they can easily scale horizontally by processing multiple requests concurrently. However, to scale effectively, you need to ensure that each function is independent and doesn't rely on any persistent state between invocations.

- **Use SQS and SNS for Event Queuing**: For asynchronous processing, use SQS or SNS to queue requests for Lambda functions, allowing multiple instances of the function to process events in parallel.
- **Load Balancing**: Use AWS API Gateway for load balancing HTTP requests. It automatically handles incoming requests and routes them to Lambda functions, scaling based on traffic volume.

3. Set Up Auto-Scaling Policies for DynamoDB and Other Services Services like DynamoDB or RDS may be part of your serverless architecture, and you need to ensure that they scale appropriately to handle growing workloads.

- **DynamoDB Auto Scaling**: Configure **DynamoDB Auto Scaling** to automatically adjust the read and write throughput of your tables based on demand. This ensures that your database can scale without manual intervention, handling varying traffic levels efficiently.
- **Use Aurora Serverless for Relational Data**: For applications requiring a relational database, **Aurora Serverless** scales automatically based on traffic and adjusts capacity on the fly, providing a cost-effective solution.

4. Implement Concurrency Control While serverless functions scale automatically, you may need to control concurrency to ensure that resources are used efficiently and that services don't overwhelm downstream systems.

- **Reserved Concurrency for Critical Functions**: Set **reserved concurrency** for Lambda functions that need to handle a fixed number of requests simultaneously. This prevents functions from consuming more resources than needed, avoiding the risk of overwhelming your system.

- **Provisioned Concurrency**: Use **Provisioned Concurrency** to ensure that critical Lambda functions are pre-warmed and ready to handle traffic without cold start latency.

5. Monitor and Adjust Based on Metrics Serverless applications scale based on traffic and resource utilization. Monitoring is crucial to ensure your functions are scaling correctly and cost-effectively. Use metrics from CloudWatch, X-Ray, and other monitoring tools to track performance and adjust configurations.

- **Monitor Invocation Rates**: Track Lambda invocation rates, durations, error rates, and concurrent executions. If invocation rates increase, ensure that your system can scale by adjusting function concurrency or invoking more instances of your services.
- **Track Resource Consumption**: Monitor memory, CPU usage, and timeouts to optimize resource usage and ensure that scaling is done efficiently.

6. Implement API Gateway for Traffic Management API Gateway can act as a traffic manager for your serverless microservices, allowing you to implement features such as rate limiting, throttling, and caching to optimize scaling.

- **Throttling and Rate Limiting**: Set up throttling to control the number of requests that your services handle per second. This prevents overwhelming your system during traffic surges and helps ensure reliable scaling.
- **Caching**: Implement caching in API Gateway to reduce the load on your Lambda functions and speed up response times for frequently accessed data.

By designing for independence, using proper scaling mechanisms, and continuously monitoring and adjusting, your serverless microservices will scale effectively and efficiently.

9.6 Monitoring and Managing Serverless Costs

While serverless architectures offer a pay-as-you-go pricing model, monitoring and managing costs are essential to avoid unexpected charges, especially in large-scale environments. Here are key strategies to manage and monitor serverless costs effectively:

1. Understand AWS Lambda Pricing AWS Lambda charges are based on the number of requests and the execution time of functions, with charges calculated based on the allocated memory for each function. The more memory and execution time your function consumes, the higher the cost. To optimize costs:

- **Optimize Memory Allocation**: Adjust memory allocation based on the actual needs of your function. Increasing the memory can reduce execution time, but it also increases cost. Use CloudWatch metrics to monitor function performance and find the optimal memory allocation.
- **Reduce Execution Time**: Optimize the function logic to ensure that it completes as quickly as possible, reducing the execution time and thus the cost. Minimize external dependencies and optimize code for faster execution.

2. Use the Free Tier and Optimize Function Execution AWS offers a free tier for Lambda, which includes 1 million requests and 400,000 GB-seconds of compute time per month. By staying within the free tier, you can significantly reduce your Lambda costs if your traffic volume is low.

- **Take Advantage of the Free Tier**: For low-traffic applications, ensure that you take full advantage of the free tier to minimize costs. Track your usage in AWS Cost Explorer to stay within the free limits.
- **Monitor Cold Starts**: Cold starts add latency and execution time to Lambda functions, which can increase costs. Use **Provisioned Concurrency** to keep critical functions warm, and adjust cold start times by optimizing the initialization logic of your Lambda functions.

3. Implement Cost Controls for Data and API Services Serverless applications rely on various AWS services (e.g., API Gateway, SQS, DynamoDB) that incur additional costs based on usage. To manage costs effectively:

- **API Gateway**: API Gateway charges based on the number of API calls and the amount of data transferred. Use throttling and rate-limiting to control traffic and prevent excessive API calls. Enable caching to reduce the number of calls to Lambda and improve performance.
- **DynamoDB**: DynamoDB offers both provisioned and on-demand capacity modes. If your traffic is unpredictable, use **on-demand mode** to avoid over-provisioning resources. Monitor read and write throughput usage with CloudWatch to ensure you're not over-provisioning.
- **SQS and SNS**: For event-driven architectures, services like **SQS** and **SNS** charge based on the number of requests and the amount of data transferred. Monitor the usage of these services to avoid unexpected costs.

4. Use Cost Explorer and Budget Alerts AWS **Cost Explorer** allows you to analyze cost trends and identify areas where your serverless functions are generating high costs. Set up **AWS Budgets** to monitor and alert you when your usage or costs exceed a defined threshold.

- **Cost Explorer**: Use Cost Explorer to drill down into the cost data and identify which Lambda functions, services, or resources are incurring the highest charges.
- **Budget Alerts**: Set up budget alerts to receive notifications when your spending exceeds predefined limits. This helps you stay on top of potential cost overruns and take corrective action before costs escalate.

5. Optimize Storage Costs In serverless applications, storage services such as **S3**, **DynamoDB**, and **EFS** are commonly used. Each service has its own pricing model, so optimizing storage costs is important.

- **S3**: If you're storing large amounts of data in **Amazon S3**, consider using lifecycle policies to automatically archive or delete older data that is no longer needed. Use **S3 Intelligent-Tiering** to optimize storage costs by moving objects to the most cost-effective storage class.
- **DynamoDB**: If you're storing large amounts of data in **DynamoDB**, monitor read and write capacity to avoid over-provisioning. For infrequently accessed data, consider using **DynamoDB on-demand** mode to reduce costs.

By continuously monitoring resource usage and leveraging cost optimization features in AWS, you can effectively manage and reduce costs associated with serverless applications.

9.7 Scaling Serverless Functions Automatically

One of the most powerful benefits of serverless architectures is the automatic scaling of functions based on demand. However, to maximize the potential of serverless scaling, it's essential to understand how AWS Lambda and other serverless resources automatically scale and how you can configure them to meet your specific needs.

1. Auto-Scaling in AWS Lambda AWS Lambda automatically scales by launching new instances of your function in response to incoming events. When a function is invoked, Lambda allocates resources dynamically based on the incoming traffic.

- **Event Sources**: Lambda functions can be triggered by various AWS event sources, including API Gateway, SQS, SNS, DynamoDB Streams, and more. When an event occurs, Lambda scales the number of function instances based on the event volume, processing each event concurrently.
- **Concurrency Scaling**: Lambda automatically scales the concurrency of your functions based on demand. The more requests Lambda receives, the more instances it will launch to process the requests concurrently, without requiring you to manage scaling manually.

2. Use Reserved and Provisioned Concurrency for Critical Functions For critical functions that need to handle high traffic or require low-latency processing, you can configure **reserved concurrency** or **provisioned concurrency**.

- **Reserved Concurrency**: Reserved concurrency guarantees a specific number of concurrent function executions. This ensures that your function always has the necessary resources to handle traffic, even during high-demand periods.
- **Provisioned Concurrency**: Provisioned concurrency ensures that a specific number of Lambda instances are always pre-warmed and ready to handle traffic. This reduces cold start latency and guarantees that your function can handle traffic spikes instantly.

3. Use Amazon API Gateway for Load Balancing API Gateway can handle the load balancing for Lambda functions when they are invoked via HTTP requests. It automatically routes incoming traffic to Lambda functions and manages throttling, rate limiting, and scaling.

- **Throttling and Rate Limiting**: API Gateway can be configured to throttle traffic and set rate limits for specific endpoints. This helps manage traffic spikes and ensures that Lambda functions are not overwhelmed during periods of high traffic.
- **Caching**: Enable caching in API Gateway to reduce the load on Lambda functions by caching frequently accessed data at the API Gateway level.

4. Event-Driven Scaling with SQS and SNS When using **SNS** or **SQS** to trigger Lambda functions, these services can automatically scale to handle the volume of incoming messages.

- **SQS Queue Scaling**: SQS queues automatically scale to handle large volumes of messages. When a message is added to the queue, Lambda automatically reads and processes the messages in parallel based on the number of available instances.

149

- **SNS Topic Scaling**: SNS can trigger multiple Lambda functions concurrently based on the number of subscribers, ensuring that messages are processed in parallel.

5. Horizontal Scaling for Other Serverless Services For other services like **DynamoDB**, **RDS**, and **S3**, horizontal scaling ensures that your application can handle increased load automatically.

- **DynamoDB Auto Scaling**: DynamoDB automatically adjusts throughput based on usage patterns, ensuring that your application can scale without manual intervention.
- **RDS Aurora Serverless**: **Aurora Serverless** automatically adjusts the database's compute capacity based on demand, scaling up during high load and scaling down when demand decreases.

Chapter 10: Future of Serverless and Microservices

10.1 Emerging Trends in Serverless Computing

Serverless computing has rapidly evolved and continues to shape the way developers approach application design and infrastructure management. As serverless technology matures, several emerging trends are expected to have a significant impact on the future of serverless computing.

1. Increased Adoption of Multi-Cloud and Hybrid Cloud Architectures One of the key trends in serverless computing is the increasing adoption of **multi-cloud** and **hybrid cloud** environments. Organizations are moving away from a single-cloud approach, choosing to use multiple cloud providers or a mix of on-premise and cloud-based resources. This flexibility allows organizations to avoid vendor lock-in and choose the best tools for their specific needs.

- **Serverless on Multiple Cloud Providers**: While AWS Lambda has been the dominant player, other cloud providers like **Google Cloud Functions**, **Azure Functions**, and **IBM Cloud Functions** are also becoming widely adopted. The future will see more seamless integration of serverless services across these cloud providers.
- **Hybrid Serverless Architectures**: Organizations may also use on-premises servers combined with serverless functions running on the cloud. This hybrid approach allows them to maintain certain workloads on-prem while scaling others in the cloud, providing the benefits of serverless computing without compromising on security or data residency requirements.

2. Serverless for Stateful Applications While serverless functions are traditionally stateless, there is a growing trend toward using serverless for stateful applications. Stateful applications require some form of persistence between requests, which has historically been challenging in serverless environments due to Lambda's stateless nature.

- **Stateful Serverless Functions**: Services like **AWS Step Functions** and **AWS Lambda** are evolving to allow better support for stateful workflows. By integrating state management into the orchestration layer, serverless architectures can handle more complex use cases such as long-running processes or applications that require session persistence.
- **Serverless Databases and Storage**: Innovations in serverless databases like **Amazon Aurora Serverless**, **Google Cloud Firestore**, and **DynamoDB Streams** are paving the way for more seamless integration of stateful services with serverless functions, enabling the creation of highly scalable, stateful applications without sacrificing performance or flexibility.

3. Serverless for Machine Learning and AI Workloads Serverless computing is also making its way into machine learning and AI applications. Traditionally, machine learning models have been complex to deploy and manage, often requiring dedicated infrastructure. However, serverless functions are beginning to offer a new way to scale machine learning workloads more easily.

- **Serverless AI**: Platforms like **AWS SageMaker**, **Google AI**, and **Azure AI** are beginning to integrate serverless capabilities, allowing developers to run AI models without managing the underlying infrastructure. This allows for elastic scaling based on demand and eliminates the need for manual provisioning of resources.

4. Event-Driven Serverless Architectures Serverless applications are naturally event-driven, and the trend towards **event-driven architectures** is gaining momentum. The rise of IoT, real-time data processing, and microservices has created an environment where event-driven programming is becoming more prominent.

- **Event Streaming and Serverless**: With the growing popularity of technologies like **Apache Kafka**, **AWS Kinesis**, and **Google Pub/Sub**, serverless functions can be easily triggered by real-time events from different sources. This event-driven model enables more dynamic and flexible applications, particularly in industries like finance, e-commerce, and IoT, where real-time data processing is critical.

5. Increased Use of Serverless Frameworks and Tools The rise of serverless computing has led to the development of various frameworks and tools that streamline the deployment, monitoring, and management of serverless applications. These tools are becoming more sophisticated and will continue to evolve in the coming years.

- **Serverless Framework**: As the most popular open-source tool for building and deploying serverless applications, the **Serverless Framework** is expected to continue growing in popularity. It simplifies the process of deploying Lambda functions, managing APIs, and orchestrating workflows across services.
- **Other Tools**: Tools like **AWS SAM**, **CloudFormation**, **Terraform**, and **Kubeless** provide developers with more options for managing serverless infrastructure. These frameworks and tools will continue to evolve to make it easier for organizations to deploy serverless applications at scale.

10.2 The Future of Microservices in Cloud-Native Environments

Microservices have already proven to be a game-changer in cloud-native application development. The future of microservices is closely tied to the growth of cloud-native environments, where flexibility, scalability, and automation play a crucial role.

1. Shift Towards Cloud-Native Microservices The future of microservices will involve a continued shift toward cloud-native development, where applications are built and deployed in cloud environments with a focus on scalability, resilience, and automation. Cloud-native environments leverage containerization, orchestration tools like

153

Kubernetes, and infrastructure as code (IaC) practices to deliver microservices-based applications at scale.

- **Kubernetes and Containerized Microservices**: Kubernetes has become the standard for orchestrating containerized applications in a microservices architecture. Containers provide a consistent and portable environment for running microservices, and Kubernetes helps manage the deployment, scaling, and networking of these containers across multiple nodes.
- **Cloud-Native Platforms**: Public cloud providers like AWS, Google Cloud, and Azure are investing heavily in cloud-native tools for microservices, such as **AWS Fargate** (for containerized workloads), **Google Kubernetes Engine (GKE)**, and **Azure Kubernetes Service (AKS)**. These platforms will continue to evolve, providing more efficient ways to deploy and manage microservices at scale.

2. Service Mesh for Microservices Management The growth of microservices has led to the need for advanced management tools to handle service-to-service communication, security, and observability. **Service meshes** like **Istio**, **Linkerd**, and **Consul** are becoming increasingly popular for managing microservices.

- **Service Mesh Benefits**: A service mesh provides features like traffic routing, load balancing, monitoring, security, and failure handling between microservices. This helps organizations scale their microservices architecture without sacrificing performance or security.
- **Integrated Service Meshes**: Future microservices environments will likely integrate service meshes with existing container orchestration platforms (e.g., Kubernetes), making them more seamless and easier to manage.

3. Serverless Microservices Architectures Serverless architectures and microservices are converging, as serverless functions provide an ideal model for microservices that require quick, independent scaling. Serverless microservices architectures are being adopted by organizations that want to build lightweight, scalable applications without managing the underlying infrastructure.

154

- **Serverless Containers**: **AWS Fargate**, **Google Cloud Run**, and **Azure Container Instances** are allowing microservices to be deployed in serverless environments, where the infrastructure is abstracted away but the benefits of microservices, such as isolation and scalability, are still achieved.

4. Multi-Cloud and Hybrid Architectures As organizations continue to use multiple cloud providers and on-premises data centers, there will be an increased focus on **multi-cloud** and **hybrid cloud** microservices architectures. These environments allow organizations to avoid vendor lock-in, optimize costs, and increase resilience.

- **Cloud Interoperability**: The future of microservices will see more seamless interoperability between cloud providers, allowing microservices to be distributed across different clouds. This can improve disaster recovery, enhance resilience, and optimize performance.

5. AI and Machine Learning in Microservices As machine learning and AI continue to grow, they will be integrated into microservices architectures, enabling more intelligent and autonomous systems. Microservices will be used to deploy AI models as services, making it easier to scale and manage them.

- **Microservices for AI Workloads**: The use of microservices for deploying machine learning models will grow, especially in environments where models need to be updated frequently or require high scalability. This trend will integrate AI/ML with other cloud-native technologies like Kubernetes and serverless functions for efficient scaling.

10.3 Advancements in Serverless Orchestration Tools

Serverless orchestration tools are designed to coordinate multiple serverless functions, services, and workflows in a way that simplifies application development and management. These tools are essential for building complex serverless applications that involve multiple services and processes. As serverless computing continues to evolve, the capabilities of orchestration tools are advancing to make it easier to build, scale, and monitor serverless applications.

1. Serverless Orchestration with AWS Step Functions AWS Step Functions is a serverless orchestration service that allows you to coordinate multiple AWS services into serverless workflows. It simplifies building complex applications by providing a visual workflow that integrates with services like Lambda, DynamoDB, and SNS.

- **Stateful Workflows**: Step Functions allows you to build stateful workflows that can wait for user input, retry failed tasks, or pause execution until certain conditions are met. This makes it ideal for applications that require long-running tasks or stateful behavior.

- **Integrations with Other AWS Services**: AWS Step Functions integrates with many AWS services, including Lambda, API Gateway, SQS, and SNS, making it a powerful tool for orchestrating complex serverless applications.

2. Improved Orchestration in Kubernetes-Based Serverless Architectures While Kubernetes is typically associated with containerized microservices, it is also being used for serverless orchestration. Tools like **KNative** and **Kubeless** enable serverless functionality on top of Kubernetes, providing autoscaling, event handling, and resource management.

- **KNative**: KNative is a Kubernetes-based framework that enables serverless workloads by providing features like autoscaling, traffic splitting, and event handling. It abstracts the complexity of running serverless functions while leveraging the scalability and reliability of Kubernetes.

- **Kubeless**: Kubeless is another serverless framework for Kubernetes that allows developers to run functions without worrying about the underlying infrastructure. It simplifies the deployment of serverless applications while still using Kubernetes as the underlying platform.

3. Future Trends in Orchestration Tools As the serverless ecosystem grows, orchestration tools will evolve to provide more comprehensive capabilities for developers:

- **Event-Driven Architectures**: More serverless orchestration tools will adopt event-driven architectures, allowing developers to build applications that respond to real-time events across multiple services seamlessly.
- **Cross-Cloud Orchestration**: Future orchestration tools will likely allow for cross-cloud orchestration, enabling developers to coordinate workflows across multiple cloud providers and on-premises systems without being tied to a single vendor.
- **AI-Powered Orchestration**: AI and machine learning will be increasingly integrated into serverless orchestration tools, allowing for dynamic optimization of workflows, predictive scaling, and intelligent error recovery.

10.4 The Intersection of Serverless and Edge Computing

Serverless computing and **edge computing** are two powerful paradigms that, when combined, can deliver highly efficient, scalable, and responsive applications. Edge computing focuses on processing data closer to the source of data generation, typically at the edge of a network, while serverless computing abstracts away infrastructure management, enabling developers to focus on application logic. Together, they offer compelling solutions for building fast, low-latency applications.

1. Edge Computing in Serverless Architectures The intersection of serverless and edge computing allows for more efficient data processing by running serverless functions on edge devices or at edge locations. These functions are closer to end users, resulting in reduced latency, faster processing, and a more responsive experience.

- **AWS Lambda@Edge**: AWS Lambda@Edge extends serverless computing to AWS edge locations, enabling you to run Lambda functions in response to CloudFront events closer to users. This can significantly reduce latency for content delivery and dynamic applications, such as real-time data processing, personalized content, and authentication.

- **Google Cloud Functions at the Edge**: Google Cloud offers **Cloud Functions** that can be run at the edge through **Cloud CDN**. This capability enables developers to run serverless functions closer to users, enhancing performance for globally distributed applications.

2. Benefits of Combining Serverless and Edge Computing

- **Low Latency**: By executing code closer to the user or IoT devices, you can reduce round-trip time and improve application responsiveness. This is particularly useful for applications that require real-time data processing, such as IoT, gaming, and AR/VR applications.
- **Cost Efficiency**: Edge computing reduces the need to send data back to centralized servers, saving bandwidth and processing costs. Serverless functions running at the edge incur minimal costs because they are event-driven and scale automatically, allowing for efficient use of resources.
- **Scalability**: Edge computing naturally scales across multiple locations, while serverless functions automatically scale to handle increasing traffic or data volumes. The combination ensures that both the compute and data management layers can scale seamlessly without manual intervention.

3. Real-World Use Cases

- **IoT Applications**: IoT devices generate massive amounts of data that often need to be processed locally before being sent to the cloud. Serverless functions at the edge can process and analyze this data in real-time, providing immediate insights and responses.
- **Real-Time Data Processing**: For applications that rely on real-time data, such as live video streaming or financial trading platforms, edge computing and serverless functions can process data closer to the user, reducing latency and improving performance.

- **Content Delivery and Personalization**: With Lambda@Edge and other edge computing services, content can be personalized and served from the nearest location, improving user experience by delivering fast, localized content.

10.5 The Role of Serverless in AI and Machine Learning Applications

Serverless computing is transforming how AI and machine learning (ML) models are deployed, scaled, and managed. Traditionally, machine learning applications required dedicated infrastructure and significant resources for training and inference. However, with serverless architecture, these barriers are reduced, allowing for more flexible, cost-effective, and scalable AI applications.

1. Serverless for Machine Learning Inference Serverless computing is particularly beneficial for running AI/ML models in production environments where demand fluctuates. Traditional server-based deployments require pre-provisioned resources, but with serverless, you only pay for the compute time your model needs for inference, and it automatically scales based on demand.

- **AWS Lambda for Inference**: AWS Lambda can run machine learning models for inference, processing incoming data without the need to manage infrastructure. Services like **AWS SageMaker** also integrate with Lambda to provide serverless model hosting and inference at scale.
- **Google Cloud Functions for AI**: Google Cloud Functions can be used for serverless deployment of machine learning models. Using services like **Google Cloud AI Platform**, developers can integrate serverless functions with AI/ML models to process data in real-time.

2. Serverless for Model Training While training large-scale machine learning models often requires significant resources and infrastructure, serverless computing is increasingly being used to facilitate model training, particularly for smaller models or specific tasks within the training pipeline.

159

- **AWS SageMaker with Serverless**: AWS SageMaker allows you to build, train, and deploy machine learning models using serverless compute. With **SageMaker Studio**, you can quickly spin up model training jobs on demand, and SageMaker handles the underlying infrastructure.
- **Event-Driven Training Pipelines**: Serverless architecture enables the use of event-driven pipelines for automating the process of data preprocessing, model training, and deployment. By triggering serverless functions when new data is available, you can automate the end-to-end ML pipeline and scale it easily.

3. Benefits of Serverless for AI and Machine Learning

- **Cost Efficiency**: Serverless AI/ML deployments eliminate the need for pre-provisioned infrastructure, allowing businesses to pay only for what they use. This pay-as-you-go model is especially cost-effective for workloads that require occasional or bursty computing resources.
- **Scalability**: Serverless computing scales automatically with the demands of the machine learning application. Whether you're running inference across millions of requests or processing large batches of data, serverless functions automatically scale up or down without manual intervention.
- **Faster Time to Market**: With serverless functions, deploying machine learning models becomes simpler and faster. You can quickly deploy small-scale models for testing or large-scale models for production without worrying about managing the underlying infrastructure.

4. Real-World Applications

- **Predictive Analytics**: Serverless functions can run predictive models on data streams, enabling businesses to forecast outcomes such as demand, sales, or customer behavior in real-time.
- **Natural Language Processing (NLP)**: Serverless functions can be used to process and analyze large volumes of text data for sentiment analysis, chatbots, and language translation, without the need for dedicated infrastructure.

160

- **Computer Vision**: Serverless computing is particularly useful for running image and video processing models, which can scale dynamically depending on the volume of incoming media.

10.6 How to Stay Ahead in the Serverless Space: Continuous Learning and Growth

The serverless ecosystem is evolving rapidly, and staying ahead of the curve requires continuous learning, experimentation, and adaptation. Here are some strategies to help you stay at the forefront of the serverless space.

1. Keep Up with New Serverless Features and Services Cloud providers are constantly adding new services and features to their serverless offerings. By staying up to date with these advancements, you can leverage the latest tools and technologies to enhance your serverless applications.

- **Follow Cloud Provider Updates**: Regularly check announcements from AWS, Google Cloud, Azure, and other cloud providers to learn about new serverless services, such as advanced event orchestration, machine learning integrations, or edge computing features.
- **Experiment with New Tools**: Once new services are announced, experiment with them in small projects to get hands-on experience and understand how they can benefit your serverless architecture.

2. Learn from the Serverless Community The serverless community is vibrant and full of experts who share their knowledge through blogs, forums, and open-source projects. Engaging with the community can provide you with valuable insights and best practices that can accelerate your learning.

- **Contribute to Open Source**: Contributing to open-source serverless projects allows you to collaborate with others, share your experiences, and learn from peers in the community.

- **Attend Conferences and Meetups**: Serverless conferences, meetups, and webinars are great opportunities to learn about new trends, tools, and strategies. Networking with other professionals can provide fresh perspectives and ideas for your own serverless applications.

3. Invest in Continuous Learning and Certifications To deepen your knowledge and stay competitive in the serverless space, invest in formal learning opportunities such as online courses, tutorials, and certifications.

- **Cloud Provider Certifications**: Many cloud providers offer certifications that focus on serverless technologies, such as **AWS Certified Solutions Architect**, **Google Professional Cloud Architect**, and **Microsoft Certified: Azure Solutions Architect Expert**. Earning certifications will give you a deeper understanding of the serverless ecosystem and increase your credibility as a cloud professional.
- **Online Courses and Tutorials**: Platforms like **Coursera**, **Udemy**, and **A Cloud Guru** offer in-depth courses on serverless computing and cloud-native technologies. These courses can help you stay ahead of the curve with practical skills and knowledge.

4. Build Real-World Serverless Applications To truly understand the potential of serverless computing, build real-world applications that incorporate serverless technologies. Whether it's a small project or a large-scale production system, hands-on experience is the best way to learn.

- **Start with Simple Projects**: Begin by building small, event-driven serverless applications that incorporate services like AWS Lambda, DynamoDB, and API Gateway.
- **Scale to Complex Systems**: As you gain more experience, move toward larger, more complex serverless applications, such as microservices-based systems or real-time data processing pipelines.

5. Follow Thought Leaders and Industry Experts Stay connected with thought leaders in the serverless space by following their blogs, social media, and talks. Many experts share valuable insights on the latest serverless trends, best practices, and case studies.

- **Top Thought Leaders**: Follow industry leaders like **Jeremy Daly**, **Mike Roberts**, **Danilo Poccia**, and others who share in-depth insights and practical advice on serverless computing.

Chapter 11: Conclusion and Next Steps

11.1 Summarizing Key Takeaways from the Book

Throughout this book, we've explored the world of **serverless computing** and **microservices** in depth, uncovering their benefits, challenges, and how they are transforming the way applications are built and scaled. Here are the key takeaways:

1. Serverless Computing Enables Simplicity and Scalability Serverless computing abstracts away infrastructure management, enabling developers to focus solely on application logic. This shift to event-driven, stateless architectures allows applications to scale automatically based on demand, without the need for provisioning or maintaining servers. With serverless, you pay only for the compute resources used, making it a cost-efficient solution for many workloads.

2. Microservices and Serverless Go Hand-in-Hand Microservices architectures break down applications into smaller, independent services that communicate over well-defined APIs. Combining serverless with microservices allows organizations to build scalable, maintainable, and cost-effective applications. Each microservice can scale independently, improving both performance and resilience.

3. Event-Driven and Serverless Architectures are the Future Event-driven architectures are becoming increasingly popular in serverless environments, allowing applications to respond to real-time data and changes. Using services like **AWS Lambda**, **SNS**, **SQS**, and **EventBridge**, developers can create event-driven systems that are both flexible and scalable, without relying on tightly coupled components.

4. Serverless and Edge Computing Provide Low-Latency Solutions The integration of serverless computing with edge computing allows for data processing closer to users, reducing latency and improving the performance of real-time applications like IoT, gaming, and personalized content delivery. **Lambda@Edge** and similar services offer the ability to run serverless functions at the edge, significantly enhancing the user experience.

5. Serverless for AI and Machine Learning Serverless computing is transforming AI and machine learning by providing scalable infrastructure for running models without the need to manage servers. With serverless, machine learning inference can be run in real-time or in response to specific events, making it easier to integrate AI capabilities into applications with minimal overhead.

6. Cost Optimization and Performance Tuning are Crucial While serverless architectures are cost-effective, managing costs requires understanding how pricing works and continuously optimizing the performance of your functions. By fine-tuning function execution times, memory allocation, and resource utilization, you can keep costs under control while ensuring your application remains responsive.

7. Tools and Frameworks are Evolving The serverless ecosystem continues to evolve, with new tools and frameworks emerging to simplify the development, deployment, and monitoring of serverless applications. The **Serverless Framework**, **AWS SAM**, and **Kubernetes-based serverless solutions** are making it easier for developers to build and manage serverless applications at scale.

8. The Future is Multi-Cloud, Hybrid, and Distributed As organizations move toward multi-cloud and hybrid cloud environments, serverless computing will play a pivotal role in managing workloads across various cloud platforms. The flexibility and portability of serverless architectures will allow applications to run across different providers and on-premises environments, reducing vendor lock-in and increasing resilience.

11.2 How to Continue Your Serverless Journey

The world of serverless computing is continuously evolving, and there are many ways you can continue to grow and expand your knowledge. Here are some key next steps for anyone looking to further their understanding and expertise in serverless technologies:

1. Get Hands-On Experience with Serverless Projects The best way to learn serverless computing is to apply what you've learned by building real-world projects. Start by developing small applications and gradually tackle more complex systems as you become more comfortable with serverless tools and frameworks.

- **Experiment with AWS Lambda, API Gateway, and DynamoDB**: Build APIs using Lambda and API Gateway, and store data in DynamoDB. This will give you a hands-on understanding of how serverless components work together.
- **Try Event-Driven Applications**: Create event-driven applications that process data from sources like SQS, SNS, or Kinesis, and explore how to scale these applications dynamically.

2. Dive Deeper into Serverless Frameworks and Tools As you become more experienced, explore different serverless frameworks that can simplify deployment and management. Consider experimenting with frameworks like the **Serverless Framework**, **AWS SAM**, and **Google Cloud Functions** to streamline your serverless development process.

- **Learn Serverless Orchestration**: Explore tools like **AWS Step Functions** and **AWS EventBridge** to create complex workflows and automate processes across multiple serverless functions.

3. Explore Advanced Topics in Serverless Computing To stay ahead in the serverless space, dive into advanced topics such as:

- **Serverless at Scale**: Learn how to manage large-scale serverless applications, including techniques for optimizing performance, managing state, and integrating with databases and storage services.
- **Serverless Security**: Serverless applications present unique security challenges, such as ensuring the secure execution of functions and handling sensitive data. Learn about best practices for securing serverless applications and integrating with IAM and other security services.

4. Keep Up with Industry Trends and Updates Serverless computing is a fast-moving space, with cloud providers continually releasing new features and tools. To stay current:

- **Follow Blogs and News**: Subscribe to blogs like **AWS News, Serverless.com**, and **Google Cloud Platform Blog** to keep up with the latest developments in serverless technology.
- **Join the Serverless Community**: Engage with the serverless community by participating in forums, webinars, and meetups. Many conferences, such as **ServerlessConf**, focus specifically on serverless computing, offering deep insights into industry trends and best practices.

5. Get Certified in Serverless Technologies If you want to deepen your knowledge and demonstrate your expertise, consider pursuing cloud certifications focused on serverless architectures. AWS, Google Cloud, and Azure all offer certifications that cover serverless technologies in detail.

- **AWS Certified Solutions Architect – Associate**: This certification focuses on designing and deploying applications on AWS, including serverless architectures.
- **Google Cloud Professional Cloud Architect**: This certification covers serverless and cloud-native application development on Google Cloud.

- **Microsoft Certified: Azure Solutions Architect Expert**: This certification covers designing and implementing solutions on Azure, including serverless and microservices architectures.

6. Contribute to Open-Source Serverless Projects Contributing to open-source serverless projects allows you to gain experience working with cutting-edge technologies while giving back to the community. Open-source contributions help you build your portfolio, collaborate with others, and stay on the pulse of the latest serverless developments.

7. Stay Curious and Experiment with New Technologies Serverless computing is constantly evolving, and staying curious is key to mastering it. Explore new serverless offerings from cloud providers, try integrating serverless with new technologies (like edge computing and machine learning), and experiment with new architectures as they emerge.

By following these next steps, you can continue to build on your knowledge of serverless computing and microservices, ensuring that you stay at the forefront of this rapidly evolving field. Whether you're building small projects or managing large-scale production systems, serverless computing offers endless opportunities to create scalable, efficient, and cost-effective applications.

11.3 Joining the Serverless Community: Forums, Meetups, and Events

Becoming an active member of the serverless community is one of the best ways to stay up-to-date with the latest trends, connect with fellow developers, and continue learning. The serverless ecosystem is rapidly evolving, and engaging with the community will help you stay informed and gain valuable insights. Here are some great ways to join the serverless community:

1. Online Forums and Communities

Online forums and communities provide platforms for asking questions, sharing knowledge, and collaborating with others. Some popular places to get involved include:

- **Serverless Framework Slack Channel**: Join the official **Serverless Framework** Slack channel to connect with other developers, ask questions, and engage in discussions about best practices and troubleshooting serverless challenges.
- **Stack Overflow**: The serverless tag on **Stack Overflow** is full of useful questions and answers about common issues, tools, and architectures in serverless development.
- **Reddit**: Subreddits like **r/serverless** are great places to discuss serverless technologies, share resources, and stay informed about industry trends.

2. Meetups and Local Groups Joining meetups and local communities allows you to connect with other serverless enthusiasts in your area. Many meetups host events, hackathons, and talks on serverless technologies.

- **Meetup.com**: Search for serverless-related meetups in your area. Whether it's AWS Lambda, microservices, or serverless security, you'll find opportunities to meet others with similar interests.
- **Local User Groups**: Some cities host serverless-specific or cloud-focused user groups. These are excellent venues to learn from experienced practitioners, network with peers, and attend talks by industry leaders.

3. Serverless Conferences and Events Attending conferences and events is one of the best ways to immerse yourself in the world of serverless computing. These events typically feature presentations by industry experts, hands-on workshops, and opportunities to network with other professionals.

- **ServerlessConf**: This is one of the most well-known conferences focused specifically on serverless technologies. It features expert speakers, workshops, and deep dives into the latest serverless trends.
- **AWS re:Invent**: AWS re:Invent is AWS's annual conference where developers, engineers, and cloud professionals gather to learn about the latest AWS services, including Lambda and other serverless technologies.
- **Google Cloud Next**: Google's flagship event, **Cloud Next**, includes sessions on serverless computing, Google Cloud Functions, and other cloud-native technologies.

4. Online Events and Webinars If attending in-person events isn't an option, there are plenty of **webinars** and **online events** that allow you to engage with the serverless community virtually. Many cloud providers and serverless-focused companies regularly host online events, workshops, and tutorials.

- **AWS webinars and live streams**: AWS frequently offers online tutorials, Q&A sessions, and deep dives into serverless products like Lambda, Step Functions, and API Gateway.
- **ServerlessConf Virtual**: If you can't attend ServerlessConf in person, the event offers a virtual version where you can access recorded sessions and live streams.

5. Participate in Open-Source Projects Contributing to open-source projects in the serverless space is a great way to connect with other developers, gain experience with cutting-edge technologies, and make meaningful contributions to the community.

- **Contribute to Serverless Framework**: The **Serverless Framework** itself is open source, and contributing to it is an excellent way to engage with the community and help shape the future of serverless development.
- **GitHub Projects**: Many serverless tools and frameworks are hosted on GitHub. Contributing to these projects, fixing bugs, or adding features can help you become more involved in the serverless ecosystem.

By joining these communities, attending events, and contributing to open-source projects, you'll stay connected, learn from others, and continue to grow your expertise in serverless computing.

11.4 Final Thoughts on the Future of Serverless Microservices

The future of serverless microservices looks incredibly promising. Serverless computing has already revolutionized the way we build, deploy, and scale applications, and as the technology matures, we can expect even more innovations and opportunities.

1. Evolution of Serverless Tools and Frameworks

The tools and frameworks available for building and managing serverless microservices will continue to evolve. With platforms like **AWS Lambda**, **Azure Functions**, and **Google Cloud Functions**, cloud providers are adding more features and integrations to make serverless computing even more accessible, cost-effective, and powerful.

Serverless frameworks like the **Serverless Framework** and **AWS SAM** are also evolving to make development and deployment even more efficient, providing better integration with infrastructure as code (IaC), monitoring, and debugging tools.

2. Integration with AI, Edge Computing, and IoT

Serverless computing is increasingly being used to power real-time data processing applications, from AI and machine learning models to edge computing and IoT. These technologies are becoming more integrated with serverless architectures, allowing developers to build highly scalable, distributed, and low-latency applications that process data at the edge or in real-time.

3. Hybrid and Multi-Cloud Architectures

As businesses continue to adopt hybrid and multi-cloud strategies, serverless architectures will play a central role in enabling cross-cloud and hybrid applications. Serverless microservices can run seamlessly across multiple cloud providers, offering businesses the flexibility to optimize costs, reduce vendor lock-in, and ensure resilience across different environments.

4. Serverless for Complex Applications

What began as a way to manage simple workloads is now evolving into a solution for more complex applications. With advancements in serverless orchestration tools like **AWS Step Functions**, **Google Cloud Pub/Sub**, and **Azure Logic Apps**, serverless computing can now be used to build and manage sophisticated workflows that coordinate multiple services.

In the future, we'll see serverless becoming the default architecture for many large-scale, high-performance applications, enabling businesses to build powerful systems while keeping complexity and operational overhead to a minimum.

5. The Democratization of Computing

Serverless computing lowers the barriers to entry for developers by abstracting away infrastructure management and reducing the cost of running applications. As the technology becomes more mature and widespread, we will see an increase in the democratization of computing. Startups, individual developers, and smaller organizations will have access to the same powerful tools and resources as large enterprises, enabling innovation at all levels.

Serverless microservices will continue to transform industries and enable new, innovative applications that were previously difficult or expensive to build. The future is bright for serverless computing, and those who embrace it will have a competitive edge in building the next generation of applications.

11.5 Resources for Further Reading and Learning

To continue your learning journey and deepen your expertise in serverless computing and microservices, here are some excellent resources:

1. Books

- **"Serverless Architectures on AWS"** by Peter Sbarski: A comprehensive guide to building serverless applications on AWS, covering everything from Lambda to API Gateway and DynamoDB.
- **"The Serverless Framework"** by Yan Cui: This book dives deep into using the Serverless Framework, an open-source tool for building serverless applications.
- **"Designing Data-Intensive Applications"** by Martin Kleppmann: While not solely focused on serverless, this book provides valuable insights into building data-intensive applications, which is crucial when working with microservices and serverless architectures.

2. Online Courses

- **AWS Training and Certification**: AWS offers numerous courses focused on serverless computing, including **AWS Lambda** and **AWS SAM**.
- **Serverless Framework Courses**: The **Serverless Framework** offers a free course on their website to help you get started with building serverless applications.
- **Coursera – Serverless Architectures**: This course covers various aspects of serverless architectures, including event-driven programming and cloud-native development.

3. Blogs and Tutorials

- **Serverless.com Blog**: The official blog for the Serverless Framework is full of tutorials, industry insights, and best practices for working with serverless architectures.
- **AWS Compute Blog**: AWS regularly publishes blog posts about Lambda, Step Functions, and other serverless technologies. It's a great resource to keep up-to-date with new features and practical tips.

- **Medium – Serverless Articles**: Medium hosts a wide range of articles written by experts in the field of serverless computing. Look for articles tagged with "serverless" or "AWS Lambda" for the latest trends, tutorials, and case studies.

4. Documentation

- **AWS Lambda Documentation**: The official documentation for AWS Lambda includes detailed information on how to get started, best practices, and advanced use cases.
- **Google Cloud Functions Documentation**: Google's official documentation provides in-depth guides and examples on using Cloud Functions to build serverless applications on the Google Cloud Platform.
- **Serverless Framework Documentation**: The official documentation for the Serverless Framework includes extensive guides, tutorials, and references to help you deploy serverless applications.

By utilizing these resources, you can continue your serverless journey and stay ahead in this rapidly evolving field.

Appendices

A.1 Glossary of Key Terms

Here's a glossary of important terms and concepts discussed throughout this book. Understanding these key terms will help you navigate the world of serverless and microservices architectures with ease.

- **API Gateway**: A service that acts as a single entry point for client requests to backend services, often used in serverless architectures to route HTTP requests to AWS Lambda functions or other services.
- **AWS Lambda**: A serverless computing service provided by Amazon Web Services that runs code in response to events without the need for managing servers. Functions are stateless and can scale automatically based on demand.
- **Microservices**: A software architecture pattern where an application is divided into small, independent services, each responsible for a specific piece of functionality. These services communicate over well-defined APIs and can be deployed and scaled independently.
- **Serverless**: A cloud computing model where the cloud provider manages infrastructure, scaling, and resource allocation. Developers only need to deploy their code, which is executed in response to events (e.g., HTTP requests, file uploads, etc.).
- **Event-Driven Architecture**: An architectural pattern where services react to events or changes in data. This is a natural fit for serverless applications, where functions are triggered by events such as API calls, database updates, or message queues.
- **Provisioned Concurrency**: A feature in AWS Lambda that allows you to pre-warm a specified number of function instances, eliminating cold start latency for critical applications.

- **DynamoDB**: A fully managed NoSQL database provided by AWS, commonly used in serverless applications to store and retrieve data in a highly scalable manner.
- **Step Functions**: An AWS service for orchestrating workflows between AWS services, enabling complex processes to be managed and executed in a coordinated, stateful manner.
- **Service Mesh**: A dedicated infrastructure layer for handling communication between microservices, often used to manage traffic, security, and observability across services.
- **Cold Start**: The delay introduced when a serverless function is invoked for the first time or after a period of inactivity. Cold starts occur because the cloud provider needs to initialize the function's environment before execution.
- **Concurrency**: The number of simultaneous executions of a serverless function. Managing concurrency ensures that functions can handle large volumes of incoming requests without overloading resources.
- **CI/CD**: Continuous Integration and Continuous Deployment are practices that involve automatically testing and deploying code changes to production systems. In serverless applications, CI/CD pipelines streamline the process of deploying Lambda functions and other cloud services.
- **Serverless Framework**: An open-source framework for building and deploying serverless applications. It simplifies the process of creating Lambda functions, APIs, and other cloud resources.
- **Containerization**: The process of packaging applications and their dependencies into containers, allowing them to run consistently across different environments. In serverless computing, containers are often used to deploy workloads on platforms like **AWS Fargate** and **Google Cloud Run**.

A.2 Recommended Tools and Libraries for Serverless Microservices

When building serverless microservices, having the right set of tools and libraries can greatly improve development efficiency and application performance. Here are some tools and libraries that are particularly useful for serverless applications:

1. Serverless Framework

- **Description**: A widely used open-source framework for building and deploying serverless applications. It simplifies the management of cloud functions, APIs, and other serverless resources.
- **Website**: https://www.serverless.com/

2. AWS SAM (Serverless Application Model)

- **Description**: AWS SAM is an open-source framework designed to make it easier to build and deploy serverless applications on AWS. It integrates directly with AWS CloudFormation for infrastructure-as-code management.
- **Website**: https://aws.amazon.com/serverless/sam/

3. LocalStack

- **Description**: A fully functional local AWS cloud stack that simulates AWS services locally for development and testing. It supports services like Lambda, S3, DynamoDB, and more.
- **Website**: https://localstack.cloud/

4. AWS Chalice

- **Description**: A Python-based framework for building serverless applications, particularly useful for AWS Lambda and API Gateway integration. It's a lightweight alternative to the Serverless Framework for simpler Python-based applications.

- **Website**: https://chalice.aws.amazon.com/

5. DynamoDB Local

- **Description**: A local version of AWS DynamoDB that can be run on your machine for offline development and testing. It's useful for simulating DynamoDB operations without needing access to the cloud.
- **Website**: https://docs.aws.amazon.com/amazondynamodb/latest/developerguide/DynamoDBLocal.html

6. AWS X-Ray

- **Description**: A service that helps with debugging and analyzing serverless applications by providing distributed tracing. X-Ray allows you to trace requests and visualize their flow through various AWS services, helping to diagnose performance issues.
- **Website**: https://aws.amazon.com/xray/

7. AWS CloudFormation

- **Description**: An infrastructure-as-code (IaC) service that allows you to define AWS resources using JSON or YAML templates. CloudFormation helps automate the provisioning and management of serverless components like Lambda functions, API Gateway, and DynamoDB.
- **Website**: https://aws.amazon.com/cloudformation/

8. Terraform

- **Description**: A popular IaC tool that supports multi-cloud environments, including AWS, Azure, and Google Cloud. Terraform allows you to define and provision serverless resources across multiple cloud providers using configuration files.

- **Website**: https://www.terraform.io/

9. Serverless-Offiline

- **Description**: A plugin for the Serverless Framework that allows you to test and develop AWS Lambda functions locally without the need to deploy them to AWS. It simulates AWS services like API Gateway and Lambda for local development.
- **Website**: https://www.npmjs.com/package/serverless-offline

10. KNative

- **Description**: An open-source platform that enables serverless workloads on Kubernetes. It offers autoscaling, event-driven architecture, and simplified management of serverless applications within Kubernetes environments.
- **Website**: https://knative.dev/

A.3 Additional Resources (Websites, Blogs, Communities)

Staying updated with the latest advancements in serverless and microservices technologies is key to your growth as a developer. Here are some additional resources for learning, networking, and staying informed:

1. Websites and Blogs

- **Serverless.com Blog**: Offers insights, tutorials, and industry updates on serverless computing and the Serverless Framework.
  - Website: https://www.serverless.com/blog
- **AWS Compute Blog**: Amazon Web Services provides articles and tutorials on serverless technologies like AWS Lambda, API Gateway, and more.
  - Website: https://aws.amazon.com/blogs/compute/
- **Google Cloud Blog**: Google's official blog for cloud-related technologies, including serverless and machine learning applications.

- Website: https://cloud.google.com/blog
- **Medium – Serverless Articles**: A great resource for finding articles on serverless computing, written by developers and thought leaders.
  - Website: https://medium.com/tag/serverless

2. Communities

- **Serverless Slack Community**: An active community where you can discuss serverless architecture, ask questions, and learn from other developers.
  - Website: https://serverless.com/slack/
- **Stack Overflow – Serverless Tag**: A popular Q&A platform where developers share solutions to serverless-related problems.
  - Website: https://stackoverflow.com/questions/tagged/serverless
- **r/serverless (Reddit)**: A subreddit dedicated to serverless technologies, where users share articles, tutorials, and questions.
  - Website: https://www.reddit.com/r/serverless/

3. Conferences and Events

- **ServerlessConf**: A global event dedicated to serverless architecture, featuring talks, workshops, and networking opportunities.
  - Website: https://www.serverlessconf.io/
- **AWS re:Invent**: AWS's annual event, which includes sessions on Lambda, serverless computing, and other cloud services.
  - Website: https://reinvent.awsevents.com/
- **Google Cloud Next**: Google's conference where serverless and cloud-native developers gather to learn about Google Cloud technologies.
  - Website: https://cloud.withgoogle.com/next

A.4 Code Snippets and GitHub Repository Access

1. GitHub Repository Access Access a curated collection of serverless code examples and best practices in this repository. These samples are designed to help you get started with common use cases, such as building APIs, data pipelines, and event-driven applications.

- **GitHub Repository for Serverless Examples**:
  https://github.com/serverless/examples

2. Example Code Snippets Here are a few snippets to help you get started with some common serverless use cases:

Lambda Function (Node.js Example):

javascript

Copy

```javascript
// Basic AWS Lambda function that processes an API request
module.exports.handler = async (event) => {
  const name = event.queryStringParameters.name || 'World';
  return {
    statusCode: 200,
    body: JSON.stringify({ message: `Hello, ${name}!` }),
  };
};
```

AWS Step Functions State Machine (JSON Example):

json

Copy

```json
{
  "StartAt": "SayHello",
```

```json
"States": {
  "SayHello": {
    "Type": "Pass",
    "Result": "Hello, World!",
    "Next": "Done"
  },
  "Done": {
    "Type": "Succeed"
  }
}
}
```

Serverless Framework serverless.yml **Example**:

yaml

Copy

```yaml
service: my-serverless-app

provider:
  name: aws
  runtime: nodejs14.x

functions:
  hello:
    handler: handler.hello
    events:
      - http:
          path: hello
          method: get
```

These code snippets provide starting points for building a simple Lambda function, a Step Functions state machine, and a basic configuration for deploying a serverless service using the **Serverless Framework**.

These appendices provide essential references to continue your serverless journey, whether you're looking for key terminology, useful tools, further learning resources, or hands-on code examples. By exploring these resources and engaging with the broader serverless community, you'll be well-equipped to build and scale powerful serverless microservices in the cloud.